FINDING YOUR
COACH

FINDING YOUR
COACH

Diving Deep Within

MELINDA J. KELLY

Finding Your Coach

Publisher:
Francis B. Kelly & Associates, Inc.

Publishing consultant:
Professional Woman Publishing LLC.
www.pwnbooks.com

ISBN: 978-0-578-20691-2

CONTENTS

INTRODUCTION

"I have come for advice."
"That is easily got."
"And help."
"That is not always so easy."

—ARTHUR CONAN DOYLE
THE FIVE ORANGE PIPS

Welcome

What do you do when you hit the crossroads? There is a reason that the word "crossroads" has endured all these years to signify transition because it feels so true no matter where your life is. When we are young, it is college or career. As we mature, it is career or family. As we get even further along, the questions become more complicated because, to my way of thinking, there isn't ever a right answer, just the one you think will make you happy … you hope will make you happy.

I found myself at those very crossroads, wondering where to go next. The desire to escape to a faraway clime was very tempting. I could tuck it all in, relocate, turn things over to a property manager and get a remote secretary for the physical things that had to be done business-wise stateside. It was all very tempting, except for learning another language and being alone, and while I am very brave about many things, I realized for this adventure, I really would prefer to have a partner in crime.

Around the same time, a family crisis ensued, and as much as I would have liked to walk away, I couldn't. It wouldn't have been true to me, and as difficult as the entire experience has been, it has taught me much about myself that I didn't know, didn't want to know, and was apprehensive to learn. I often wish I could have read a book or CliffsNotes version, but there doesn't appear to be any such creature, and so I took the real course in life. Even if there was such a resource, I don't know if I would have believed it, for without our naive belief and hope, how would we or could we ever tackle the impossible?

If you are going to have a crisis, it seems to be de rigueur that all aspects of your life implode at once, and so it was with me. Our lovely little family business that had at one time been innovative and unique, with time and technology was no longer that way. The next question was where to with that? Do I reinvent it? How would I reinvent it? What were the possibilities to reposition it? Did I want to reinvent it? Just because you have done something your entire life and are relatively good at it, does that mean you should continue? And in reinventing, are you doing it for you, for the money, or for the parent you have lost, and this was one of your strongest ties to them?

It seemed that all of my life had become about questions, about new directions, about finding out what I wanted, and I was ill prepared for that. Like many women of a certain time, I had been raised to think of family first, then others, to be aware of my actions, to bring honor to my family, organization, affiliation, and somewhere in there, be happy too.

This is not to say I have been unhappy. In many ways, I have had a very blessed, safe, fulfilled life. I have had a fair amount of accomplishments, and a wealth of people I care about and who care about me. It would be fair to say a lovely amount of travel, culture, and all the bells and whistles you hope to find along the road of life, have equally added to the mix.

Still, the questions remained, and I was stuck. Stuck in the way no one should be. More than "should I stay or should I go?" More like "what is the meaning of life?" What do I want to do? What would I like to do? What would I like to do that gives life meaning? What would I like to do that gives life meaning and might give me some financial reward, a.k.a., a different career, job, work? How do you do this when you realize that dreaming was never something encouraged in your childhood, young adulthood, and even in your recent years?

Problem solve. I can problem solve. I like to think I am a rather good problem solver. I realized, however, I was not raised to dream. For my father, dreams had led to great disappointments, and whether it was to spare us the pain he had known or to keep his loved ones near to him, dreams and hopes were not ever encouraged.

And so we come back to the questions. All the questions that continued to plague me, persist within me, return to me. I found myself looking for answers, but not yet as someone on a quest. I pursued them as someone out to solve a problem. To solve that pesky riddle that had been poking at me for days. I went to my head, instead of my heart. In finding my comfort zone in my head, I learned many valuable lessons.

First was realizing how I processed, and for me, I needed the intellectual basis, the satisfaction that this was real, tangible, logical, and practical. I needed to figure out how I had become so disconnected from myself. How was it that I had so many paths and yet felt immobilized to start on any one of them? How did I lose my advocate? My person, who no matter what, was there? And that started me down a path of inquiry. How was I, relatively well educated, relatively normal, and socially adept, completely lost when it came to me? How was it, like everyone else, I could see everything in *your* life that needed to be done, and the success that could be yours, but could not see it, feel it, believe it on my own?

So like the well-trained, fairly-good-at-it researching fiend I am, I started down a path to figure how I got so disconnected from being able to take care of my dreams, my hopes. How was it that I lost my way before I had it? And so I went to feed my mind, hoping quelling the questions there would allow my heart to quicken when the answers presented themselves to me.

Welcome to my journey, my adventure. Permit me to share the lessons I learned along the road.

Melinda J. Kelly

PART I
YOU

*He who knows others is wise;
he who knows himself is enlightened.*

—LAO TZU

Introvert or Extrovert?

Each of us thinks we know ourselves. And then we get surprised by how people introduce us to others and say things to them about the things they see in us. In other words, we all think we are transparent, but no one I know is. We all believe we are complex and mysterious, and probably to a degree, we are. I believe we are most often a reflection of our surroundings, our peers, and the environment in which we were raised. People think I am an extrovert, but I often think of myself as being introverted. I am fairly well-mannered and speak with people, but I was raised to do that. Does that make me an extrovert or polite?

Until the turn of the last century, it didn't much matter whether you were the life of the party or shy and demure. Susan Cain's work on introverts, *Quiet: The Power of Introverts in a World That Can't Stop Talking*, was a glorious eye-opener. Only recently has the extrovert taken the stage, been vaunted as a personality type to which you would want to aspire.

Thanks to Andrew Carnegie and Napoleon Hill, the salesman personality had been aspirational before that. The collection of skills and talents that were necessary for a traveling salesman— the hale-fellow-well-met personality, the knack of having a joke for any occasion, the ability to be a ready-made party guest or to talk about anything on a moment's notice—were very desirable traits. Think about the leading men of the movies through time; all too often, Mr. Staid and Steady lost the girl to Mr. Charmer.

If you are naturally an extrovert, that is great. I believe most people are somewhat introverted, but in safe situations and settings seem rather extroverted. Perhaps that is why so many people are not sure if they are an introvert or extrovert. And why do we need to categorize this, except that it seems to be human nature?

How do you know if you are an extrovert? What are the characteristics of the introvert? What are some clues, please? Here are a few questions to ask yourself. These are by no means an end-all, be-all list—just a starting place.

When I am at a party or in a social situation, I prefer to:
1   Talk with others.
2   Listen to others.

My opinion is:
1   Shared with others.
2   Kept to myself.

On a plane, I:
1   Like talking with my seatmate.
2   Hope my seatmate won't talk to me.

When I have a big decision:
1   I talk it over with people I trust.
2   I think about it and come to my own decision.

I know:
1   Most of my neighbors where I live.
2   A few of my neighbors where I live.

People see me as:
1   Outgoing and energetic.
2   Reserved and calm.

People find I am:
1   Easy to get to know.
2   Hard to get to know.

In a conversation, I tend to:
1   Speak before thinking.
2   Think before speaking.

I enjoy:
1   Social situations where I might meet new people.
2   Alone time and being by myself.

After being with a crowd of people I feel:
1   Energized.
2   Tired.

It is easy to see the pattern. If you usually selected answer A, you tend to be more extroverted. If you answered mostly B, you tend to be more introverted. If you found yourself often thinking "it depends on the situation," then you may be an introvert who can push to be an extrovert when you need to be.

I score 5 and 5, so I understand why people see me as both introverted and extroverted.

As I look at it, the question is, are you energized being around other people or do you find yourself drained after being with a group? How do you protect your energy?

Not all introverts are quiet and in their private world. *Time* magazine added a list of famous introverts to accompany their 2012 article on Susan Cain.

They listed Mohandas Gandhi (leader of the Indian independence movement), Joe DiMaggio (Baseball Hall of Famer), Moses (religious leader), Warren Buffett and Bill Gates (investors and philanthropists), and Mother Teresa (nun and missionary.) Interesting to note that each has influenced the world in different ways.

The article also included extroverts: politicians Bill Clinton, Winston Churchill, George W. Bush, Margaret Thatcher, and Boris Yeltsin, and boxer and activist, Muhammad Ali. I believe we see a trend here. To go on the road and shake that many hands, you would need to be an extrovert!

Introverts approach situations a little nervously, a little gingerly, or, one might say, with high hopes and a fair degree of caution. I often say I rush slowly. It takes me time to know if I am going to go ahead or not. I need to ruminate on it for a while.

Now for extroverts, the hale-fellow-well-met, the world-is-their-oyster, "I bounce when I walk," ever-so-happy campers. The enthusiasm with which they greet the day is also how they approach life. Extroverts are in the front row, engage in the questions, and are the participants in the room. When an extrovert's dreams and a speaker meet, they lose everything to the moment and live in the immediate. They are a coach's dream. They are an accountant's nightmare. They tend to believe everything and take advantage of opportunities that come to them.

The introvert might hesitate, but they might be right there with you, too. Just a little later.

Why ask if you are introverted or extroverted? Because knowing how you accept help or ask for help, or even process how you get help, will assist you as you begin to look at working with a coach. Extroverts will like the larger-than-life people who inspire them to greatness. Introverts might like them just as much, but need to take them in different settings. Extroverts will like big conferences and seminars, whereas introverts might like to read their book(s), take a webinar or two, and inch into the learning process.

Knowing this starting place will help you when you get to the next series of questions. The only thing you can be sure of is that this will be subject to change and review. Recently I saw that someone had coined a new term—ambivert—which means you are both. So all the answers we thought we just found might very well be out the window.

Round 2: More Questions

Working with a coach, therapist, or advisor of any kind brings forth all of our craziness, our quirks, our irrational five-year-olds within. By asking questions before we work with a professional, we can better understand how we process and where our hot spots and emotional bruises are. In the rush of daily life, taking the time to talk with ourselves isn't on the list of to-do items. We tend to spend more time looking at options for our vacations or what color paint for a room in our house. We think we know ourselves, so why would we think we needed to do this? That is what this is about, and why we seek self-help in the form of books, services, and consultations. Of course, those books often go unread. The advice offered is not taken.

Think about how you planned your last trip with a travel agent or even the woman at the auto club, and you will start to see that we are a little delusional about our knowledge on topics (new) and our ability to work effortlessly with people (old habits.)

I have an outrageous inner five-year-old, and she is very focused on keeping things okay enough. I didn't realize that as I started out on this process of self-help, and it could easily be argued that I wasted precious time. I believe that I began to understand what was missing and how I hadn't learned some pertinent things. Both positions are equally valid, but I prefer to see the time I spent exploring these questions as my stint at being a lab rat. I just didn't know what the expectations were for me in the maze. Now I have learned that there are all sorts of ways to do the maze, and I like that.

Back to the questions that kept coming back to me. To the reasons that no matter how much good advice I received, I was unable to act upon it, or no matter how much I thought I was ready or willing to move forward, I was still so far removed from that starting line. What are some of the most common questions? What were the questions that I realized I needed to ask myself and accept the *real* answers, not those that I hoped for?

Well, welcome to my list.

- Do you seek "parental" approval?
- Do you need to be the nice person?
- Do you need to be the smart person?
- Do you have issues with authority figures?
- Do you need to be loved?
- Do you need to have everyone like you?
- Do you think you are so smart already that you don't listen?

Mother?

Every one of us wants to please our parents. After all, they provide life, both literally and metaphorically. If they forgot to feed us, we went hungry. When we were babies, if they didn't pick us up when we cried, we felt unloved or not worthy. At a young age, we learned to appease the power, the nurturer, and the giver. It is a lifelong lesson. But we need to question and rethink a few things as we approach adulthood. As children, we were dependent. As adults, we are no longer dependent, but we are used to doing things in a certain way, and we don't think twice about continuing to do things in that manner. This is true even when, or especially when, the habits and patterns of our lifetime might not be in our best interests; be they habits from nail biting to pacing, they have become so ingrained we don't realize we do them.

With time, we transfer the notion of "parent" to any authority figure. I don't believe we even know we are doing it. But we learn to please our parents, then our teachers, then our professors, then our bosses, then our spouses, and we do it out of love, habit, and conditioning. It makes perfect sense that unconsciously we transfer that tendency to a coach, doctor, or therapist. What's the big deal? We like to make people happy. Human nature. The catch is when we are focused on the other people, we aren't focused on ourselves. When we aren't focused on ourselves, we don't get our needs met.

When we don't get our needs met, it doesn't matter if we are doing something perfectly or fabulously, if it isn't something that is making us perfectly happy or fabulously advancing our hopes and dreams.

When we are people pleasing, we might tend to accept everything a coach tells us to do. That is part of the coaching dynamic, but it is important to be in the conversation. Coaches see things from many angles and are puzzling things out with you and for you. Each dream is different, and it is important that as you are achieving your hopes and dreams that they stay true to your vision. You might want to go slowly, and your coach might believe you need to go quicker. There is no right answer. Perhaps they are right in the long run, and you should jump on an opportunity, but conversely, if you are not ready for the opportunity, will you be able to capitalize on it? If you have let or led your coach to believe you are at a difference place emotionally, financially, or businesswise than you are, you are not being fair to either of you. Another way to see it is if you have perfected the perfect dinner mint and your family has a few diabetics; the odds may not be in your favor to receive lots of favorable responses to your creation. Plenty of people won't see your vision. When you strive only to please them or give them the respect you would give an elder or parent, you risk losing your dream.

Dreams are ethereal and need to be protected. We need to think of them as our children and protect them as we would have wished to be or were protected. And so we are back to mother once again.

Nice?

They say nice people finish last. That might be true. When we are focused on saving other people's emotions, feelings, or dreams, and don't give our honest opinions, we shortchange ourselves and others. Personally, I believe in being nice. But being nice does not mean being walked upon, or not giving your real opinion, or being steamrollered because you have trouble standing up to others. To me, being nice means knowing how to express your opinion in a way that is both honest and non-accusatory, or owning your thoughts or ideas. It's not always what you say but how you say it that matters. A gentle tone can change the direction of a conversation or help you both find what will be mutually advantageous. When we are nice and not necessarily honest about what we need—from setting a time for an appointment or accepting a task we don't want to do—we hurt others and ourselves. When we "people please" and don't give an honest answer out of deference to "nice," we don't get what we want or give other people what they might be wanting either.

If you want to schedule a meeting for Tuesday at two, and it is inconvenient for the other person, and you then acquiesce to their schedule, whose needs are being met? Tuesday fit your schedule for a variety of reasons. Did you discuss the new time and day? Or did you just defer to their schedule? Because there are few things as destructive as rushing to a meeting with someone professionally, be it in person, on a conference call, or otherwise. You may have too much going on that day and skid into the appointment by the skin of your teeth, then fly out of there the moment it is over to take care of other things. That means you lose the opportunity to process and ponder all that has been discussed, or talk with colleagues, or a million other things that can happen after a meeting. You may have shortchanged yourself first with the meeting time and again with the secondary consequences of the event. If it doesn't take care of you, then it isn't right for you, and that is our job to do for ourselves—to protect and advance ourselves.

Be nice. Discuss what works. But know if you always are working around everyone else's schedule or meeting your needs too. Your relationship with your coach will suffer for many reasons, but it is also a mirror to relationships in your life.

Perhaps those people or groups weren't so awful. You just didn't have the tools to discuss what you could do and ended up doing more than you wanted to do. To not say no, you stopped attending or helping because you weren't comfortable getting your needs addressed. You were caught up in saving the team, helping others, the classroom needs this, a million excellent reasons to give, but when we can't define our limits, sometimes we have to walk away from things we like doing. We just don't want them to become our new full-time job or part-time responsibility.

What if you are not nice? Who does it hurt? I'm not saying be mean or deliberately hurt someone. I am saying, what if you are real and directly respond "That doesn't work for me"? Negotiating within a safe environment provides you the skills and success to negotiate in other settings. If you have the tendency to say "sure," "certainly" or "that's fine," it might feel very uncomfortable to say no or to ask for your way. It also might be necessary for you to learn this new talent and flex it for a while to strengthen it, until that hoped-for magic day when you are comfortable with "Yes, I can," or "No, I cannot" or the very adult "I could help you this Tuesday from two until three." And won't that be a beautiful day?

My IQ Is Sky High

Most of us are pretty clever. Pretty smart. Pretty savvy. Often on many topics and things. This is where we fall into the problem of being the smart kid. Of being so smart, too smart, to need all this assistance. We are so busy being so clever. We don't realize we are drowning from our lack of cleverness.

In a world of knowledge, we are saying no, we have enough, even when we are paying someone to help us solve our problems. They toss us a lifeline, the life preserver, and we tell them why our swimming to the shore still makes better sense even though we are drowning. I'm not sure how this comes about. Could it be from being jumped on if you don't have or know the right answer? Or could it be from being called the answer person so often that you question how or why you would need help? Every time we are so busy having all the answers and not allowing the new knowledge in, we hurt ourselves.

We see it in so many places. From web design to social media to delegating telephone calls, we know we can do it, should do it, and want to do it. The only catch is then we stay limited by what we know at a time when everything is changing daily. As I write this, Snapchat has been discovered by the adults, and horrified, the kids are looking for the next big thing. Just like Instagram. And Facebook. And myspace. The kids find it, their parents and older people discover it, and then the movers and shakers leave for the next big thing. By the time we have it all figured out, it has changed.

Yes, we are smart, but it isn't smart to be stuck. Or to not know when it is time to let go, and I would bet we all have one story we could tell about that. It is paradoxically that ability to do it all ourselves that hurts us. Yes, we could. But that becomes another part of our journey. How well do we accept not knowing, or being shown or told that we are missing some piece of knowledge? Working with a coach is admitting that the coach has knowledge you don't have. Or that the coach has an opinion or perspective that you value and want. When we are so in love with our idea that we cannot allow any conversation about it while it is in process, we need to ask ourselves some serious questions.

Because we might find that we do drown from not taking that life preserver, and with us goes some fabulous, delightful idea, song, story, painting, business, technique—you name it.

Love Me, Please

We all want to be loved. To be liked. To be the darling of the group. If this sounds a lot like pleasing your parent, it's because it is. But this one is a little different. When coaches are working with someone, a lot of emotions come into play.

There is a degree of parent-child. Also mentor and protégé. There is an element of friendship and the trust that goes with that. There is an aspect akin to therapist and patient. Because when we are working with a coach, we are discussing our hopes and dreams. We are sharing our deepest aspirations. We are risking and trusting in ways we never thought we would, but we are.

In that risk, we are assuming depths of professional emotions, professionalism, and a degree of love, compassion, earnest affection, because when someone loves us, they won't hurt us. Yes, we all know that's not correct, but we want to, like to, think that that will be the case. Even when we are aware this sort of thinking is inappropriate, and this is a professional relationship, we still hold onto that hope. Somehow, we will be "besties."

Conversely, when we hold back and do not share our thoughts, hopes, and dreams with our coach, our mentor, it says much about us, our trust level, our sense of security, our ability or history to take emotional risks.

Don't we all just hate the realness of that remark? The truth of it all once again is this is knowledge for you, for who you are and for your comfort zone for your relationships and future. You can do anything you want. But knowing why you may not risk more will help you not only in the business aspect of your life or dreams, but in your relationships, and probably even your romantic entanglements. We hear it all the time: "With great risk comes great reward." But if the times you've risked, be it few or many, that has not been the case, how do you believe the line? Do you ask yourself "Is it me?" "Was it them?" (Which, of course, comes back down to "is it me?" since "me" picked them.) The catch is learning from the lesson presented, be it easy or hard.

The "love" question is all about your vulnerability, willingness to be vulnerable, willingness to be hurt, willingness to succeed, and willingness to try.

Each of us wants to be loved. How much are we willing to risk for our dream to become real? And if your dream is the best new widget, relationship, art, or anything, there is a deep love and protection with that dream that flavors all the surrounding relationships.

A favorite American poet of mine from the 17th century, Anne Bradstreet, expresses in "From the Author to her Book" the same hopes and fears for her work as she presents it to others. We love our work. We want others to love our work. When they do not, it is as if they are criticizing our beloved child, for, after all, it is our creation.

None of this is new, which perhaps is reassuring or perhaps disappointing, but isn't it great to know we are not alone on this journey? So in this realm of trust, love, and vulnerability, comes our truths. Most of us have been disappointed at least once. Fortunate are the few who have not been. But each time we risk, and it does not go as hoped for, we hold back a little more. We need to know how much are we holding back. We might think we have open arms when we don't at all. Until we understand our sense of vulnerability, of risk, of trust, we will gain some knowledge, but how much further could we go or could we receive if we knew where our heart lived and why it does or doesn't risk trust and love?

Y O U

Like Me

Sally Field in her famous Academy Award speech said what every person in the world has hoped for at one point in their life. "You like me. You really, really like me." What is most interesting is how we heard it and misremembered it. Ms. Field was quite precise in her language that night. "I can't deny the fact that you like me; right now, you like me."

The choice to pursue a dream is fraught with so many emotions. It is an intensely personal choice, journey, and quest. We are putting our vision out there and are asking for approval. Whether it is that perfect widget or a painting, it is ours. It is our creation, and whether we are hoping for financial gain or public acclamation, for the most part, we want to hear "We like you. We like your work." Granted there are a few out there who received their best feedback from provoking reaction or rejection, but that is only a variation on the "you like me" theme, swung around to get the feedback and reaction they wanted.

When we work with others, we need to know and be clear about our dream, our vision, and our business, and what we see as our desired result. In that, we might have to say "No thank you" to people. We might have to cut them short as they criticize or suggest changes that would make it their project.

When we are working with a coach, we have to remove that protective layer and listen. We have asked for this. We need to be open, to accept it, to listen to criticism, rejection, reworking, rephrasing, retooling, and a few other things. We asked for this. And there is a good chance we might not hear "It is perfect." At least at first, we might not hear that. This is why knowing your

17

familial relationship and your vulnerability is vital. Because right now you need to like your baby, your project, and risk hearing what might improve it, hope that the suggestions are within your comfort zone, and if not, find a way that addresses your needs to discuss it further. Since the odds, I would imagine, are highly in favor of not liking a negative reaction, or being comfortable with hearing "That is great but ..." we need to know how we accept honest, logical assessments from people whom we have asked a professional opinion. Would we be annoyed when someone points out a typo in our documents? Why are we okay with some criticism, but not all?

Maintaining the balance of the coaching relationship is a gift, even if that means saying you need time to process the suggestions and will respond the next day; such a strategy allows you to take care of you while taking care of your project. It can be hard to trust that coaches have your best interests at heart, might be seeing things further than you can at this time (which in turn might also terrify you), and are there to be your honest, unbiased sounding board. This can be especially hard to do if you have not looked at how you process things, view criticism, see support, accept suggestions, and keep your integrity. The artist's path is not easy. It is rewarding. It is wonderful. It is fraught with great highs and lows. It is almost every adjective you care to throw at it. And it is neutral. It is only how we perceive and react to remarks or suggestions that give them value. To me, the catch is knowing you like you. Your work. Your art. Your product. Your project. It may never sell. It may be a pipe dream. But you like it. You honor it. You held to your integrity. You chose your course.

The other catch is to love your work enough to see that sometimes the suggestions are not about you. Others, the professionals you have asked, are seeing what you have offered and can see it even further. They are focused on your success and accomplishment, perhaps more than what you are able to see. We take our children and pets to the doctor or vet because we know we can give them only so much. Why do we have this reluctance to accept a professional opinion here?

My hope is you did all of that and were able to accept or reject assistance from a place of strength, not a place of fear or hurt. And then when you like your project, it doesn't matter who else does. It will always be beautiful to you. The question at this point is: "Do you want it to be profitable, saleable, or seen by others?"

I Already Know

My uncle Jim used to say our family suffered from the curse of too many talents. When he first said it, I had no idea what he was talking about. As time and life have gone on, I began to appreciate his wisdom. It wasn't arrogance. It was the gift of being raised in a family where many topics, discussions, and people were part of our daily lives. Each time a new and different person showed a new way of life, it became a consideration. And we considered many things as we grew. We also grew confused.

Recently, I've seen several articles on selection fatigue. The happiest people select from a few choices, and seventy-five different breakfast cereals have altered the way we approach our morning. Even having ten different black shirts can cause us to pause in the morning as we get dressed. I saw an article about a man who limits his possessions to one 150 things. A true minimalist by any standard and hopefully a very satisfied man.

Knowledge overload can do that, too. Sometimes we are so busy being the smartest kid in the room we do not realize there are things (often many) that we do not know, and in not allowing more knowledge in, we fail ourselves. In other words, we are so smart, we are stupid. Or closed. Or blocked. Or smug. Or fill in the blank.

What it boils down to is being so full of knowledge or the illusion of knowledge and abilities that we shut down to suggestions, ideas, or anything that we haven't thought of first. We have stuffed our minds full of things, but are they the right things? Reading a recent book, I was surprised by the advice to delegate, to let go, to accept others' wisdom as being comparable to or better than yours, and that your wisdom might be in honoring what you are good and smart at doing. To return to the collective wisdom, where your special addition would be valued, and it was practical and revolutionary, and for people raised to believe they can handle it all with the help of a book, well, that was absolutely astonishing and mind boggling. We know a lot. About a lot of topics. Do we all need to hold multiple degrees in everything or is there wisdom in going to a specialist? When we can't see that asking questions of the expert is indeed being the smartest kid in the room, we accidentally keep ourselves stuck. Blocked. Closed. Smug. When did the act of accepting help, acknowledging you needed help, become a bad thing? Granted we have a DIY channel, but I am not planning on replacing my roof myself, even though they have assured me it is a very easy thing to do.

When we shut out new opinions and answers, then we have defeated what we did that was so smart in the first place. We hired someone who had the knowledge we were missing or who was helping us fine-tune our own. It is an insidious little catch 22, for all the reasons mentioned. Until we are able to let go, to trust, to see there is still more and different knowledge elsewhere, we harm ourselves. We attend events, seminars, webinars, conferences, and we hear everything. Unfortunately, very little is getting in.

What have I done? I took the word of a friend that a certain speaker was good. I went to a weekend event. I drank the Kool-Aid, took notes, loved every minute of it. I thought I was ready to go and when there was another program offered, I signed up. Within a week, I realized I had gotten caught up in the moment and wasn't sure I was ready. I ended up in the program. Certainly, I learned things and heard things. Regrettably, I was not in a place to take it all in. I like to think it came in and ruminated a bit. I very well may have been given the answer to the meaning of life, keys to the kingdom, and a host of other great things, but I was not able to fully embrace or understand them. Whose fault is that? Is there any point in finding or assigning fault? I was in over my head.

I recall a time when a scrappy six-year-old cousin was at the amusement park with me and my grandmother. Like all the younger cousins, I thought he was the sun and the moon and the stars. I loved that he was paying attention to me. However, when we ran into a friend of his from grade school. I became persona non grata, a ghost in the conversation. You can well imagine my indignation. When—to get rid of me—they went on the roller coaster (and mark my words, this was beyond tame and not like the creatures you see now!) I "ponied up" all my courage and insisted I should go, too. I survived the ride. I enjoyed the ride. I completely forgot about my cousin and his friend. I had ridden a roller coaster.

Ultimately, my experience was an okay one, even if it was a complete and total surprise to me that it would be. In my pride and anger, I was hell-bent on doing it. I survived. I learned to take a risk, and it would be okay. It's interesting for me to look back and process the whole thing. While I may have been in over my head, my reactions were clean, primal, and instantaneous. I realized my older boy cousin was in an entirely different world than I was. I was the little girl cousin, and while he might play with me at our grandmother's, he was a different person outside those doors. He was an average little boy. At that age, I am sure he was very patient and a little bored. I see this whole episode as fairly normal, rather amusing, and with time and age, probably somewhat entertaining to our parents. It also tells me I had a temper. I could be rash. I have a fair amount of moxie. I didn't and don't like being excluded. And my feelings are very sensitive. All very good things to know back then and now.

Somehow, over the years, it appears I may have lost some of that clarity or built up walls to protect myself. Either way, assigning blame does not bring the desired effect. Only clearing the confusion can take me where I need to go.

Round 3: More Questions

For those of you who thought this might be a list of sites that grant accreditation or instructions on how to research a coach in 30 minutes or less, I salute you for hanging in. This section is about how we approach the world when it is you and "me," or perhaps "them" is better. Whomever your "them" are, they will bring things from your past, your way of working with people with your own emotions. The process is normal, but when we are looking for personal growth or change, we often become focused on the goal or the promised outcome or phenomenal shift to come into our lives. We might become so focused on the desired improvement that we forget there are many steps to that place we long for. Just like marathon runners think of the finish line and their best times and often forget the early-morning and late-night runs, blisters, shin splints, and other momentary setbacks.

Looking at habits and patterns allows us to either recognize and keep them, or reassess whether they continue to serve us. Although these things may have served us in many ways in the past, the question is whether they continue to advance us. For now, the focus is on *you*. No matter how good, adequate, or amusing the coach is, if we don't know how we accept their information, how we speak their language, we are lost in the fields. We are lost dogs in high weeds. The road might be right next to us, but we cannot see it.

Now that we think we know ourselves and are ready go forth to seek assistance, this next part is about asking how we unknowingly limit ourselves. I mention all these things because I have watched myself and others do them for years. All of our lives run in cycles and circles and patterns—repeating and repeating and repeating. We often don't realize it until someone else points it out to us. These patterns can range from purchasing the same style shoe every summer to dating the same type of person, to liking the same horror movies. We get into a comfortable pattern and don't deviate from it. We feed it and feed into it every time we go to the same restaurant for a bite to eat. There are millions of restaurants, but somehow McDonald's, Applebee's and Cracker Barrel lead the list in the words that follow, "Let's get a bite to eat at …"

This section is about how we approach the world when it is you and "me," or perhaps "them" is better. Whoever your "them" is will bring things from your past, your way of working with people and working with your own emotions. The process is normal, but when we are looking for personal growth or change, we often become focused on the goal or the promised outcome or phenomenal shift to come into our lives. We might become so focused on the desired improvement, we forget there are many steps to that place we are longing for. Just like a marathon runner focuses on the finish line and her or his best time, quite often forgetting the early morning, late night runs, blisters, shin splints and other momentary setbacks.

Looking at habits and patterns allows us to either recognize and keep them, or reassess if they continue to serve us. Like all things, these have served us in many ways. The question becomes do they advance me as I am now?

It makes me think about Dante's Circles of Hell. Knowing how to navigate each level will help you in the long run. I tried to think about what the questions would be at each level. I came up with these; they ask you to take an authentic look at yourself. It doesn't help to be the smartest person in the room if you are the clueless person in the room. When we are so busy in our heads, we stop ourselves from going forward. So much of success is a belief in your hopes, your dreams, and your ideas. Add in a good fortune combined with hard, consistent work. When we are too smart for our good, we accept all the reasons to stay stuck without ever believing the possibilities and potential all around us.

Here are the seven questions I have asked myself, and I suggest you ask yourself, too:

Level I: How do I look?
Level II: What do they think of me?
Level III: How do I react to authority?
Level IV: How good is my time management?
Level V: Is this what I want or is this my distraction?
Level VI: What is my real relationship to money?
Level VII: Can I accept the responsibility for changing my life?

We've got the questions. Now let's look at how they unfold in our lives or how they did and do in my life.

Level I: How Do I Look?

The look is easy. We've all been in the seminar. We see that person who has it all going on. We are there improving our knowledge, of course. We see their professional, polished exterior and think that we would like to be them. It surprises us that they are there, seeking, when they look like they have it wired. We believe perhaps they are there as a part of the team doing the presentation, class, or lecture. We've come to this event wearing our best clothes, carrying an expensive purse, new blazer, or magic talisman that we believe makes us look like we're part of the winning team, here to just add a touch of our greatness. Some of us look hopeful. Some of us look vulnerable. Some of us look bored. But we're there.

Level I is about our external presentation; it's about wanting people to like us, believe in us, believe in us more than we may believe in ourselves. It's why we've dressed up in our best professional suits. We're hoping they believe that we're winners because we want to be winners. You can change "winners" to a business owners, entrepreneurs, or enlightened individuals. We want them to believe that we have something of value to share with the world. If clothes "make the man," we have high hopes that they will make us who we wish to be.

The catch is that exteriors change. Fashion fades. Magic talismans seem to lose power. I am not advocating abandoning social and societal norms. I am advocating coming to a place within that you can ask "the dumb question" in front of an entire room and be okay with someone rolling their eyes. It's not about them. It is about you, your search, your need, and getting to a place of comfort where you know who you are and what you bring to the table; it is pretty incredible.

Until we get there, we are attending a lecture in a foreign language we sort of speak. We'll get something out of the experience. But how much more could we have received if we had asked someone for help in understanding or someone to translate? Saving face can be very expensive. I sat for thirty minutes in the cathedral of Notre-Dame de Paris thinking I was attending High Mass. Of course, it was all in French. I speak a little embarrassing French. Enough to feel I would have the thrill of having attended Sunday Mass in France. Only the French at that time did not have an afternoon Sunday service. In my obstinacy and enthusiasm, I failed to ask if we were going to Mass. Eventually, we realized it was a lecture from a visiting bishop. A long lecture. A very long lecture. I can laugh about it now, but after forcing my way into the "service," I had to sheepishly make my exit. And then how did I look?

Which takes us to level II.

Level II: What Do They Think of Me?

We want "them" to think good things about us. We want them to believe that there is something unique to us and that they will be the ones to help us divine it. Together we will unlock the magic combination that will let us be the next Mother Teresa, Bill Gates, Oprah Winfrey, or fill-in-the-blank person of magnificence. In our hearts, we all want to be that great soul or we wouldn't be looking. We know that greatness is in there somewhere. We know we've had moments when it has risen to the surface. We know we're the smartest kids in the room and we want them to know it too. It's also why we will sign up for things we don't need, buy clothes we don't wear, take trips we don't care about, buy books we never read. We want to have the trappings of being that person, even if we aren't. Call it primal, but we want to be the bright, sparkly penny that attracts. We want to be in with the in crowd, the cool kids, the movers and shakers. We want to be with our people. Even if we aren't part of that group, tribe, movement, we want to be, and we aspire to be.

How many couch potatoes belong to the Sierra Club? Probably more than any of us realize, because the Sierra Club has positioned itself as being about more than hiking. It is about preserving the beauty and integrity of nature. Whether or not one can physically get there, or walk through it, one simply needs the desire to be part of the people who preserve beauty and nature and who effortlessly hike up hills like gazelles or mountain sheep.

The only downside to desiring mobility, as I see it, is that you must be clear on why you want to be like those people. Otherwise, no matter how much time you spend there or how many classes you take, you'll still be asking if these actions are taking you to where you need to be.

I love to eat, and love to cook, and love to take the various themed cooking classes, but I have no desire to be a gourmet or expert chef. It's fun, but not a compelling desire.

Are you looking for someone or something to advance your social media presence, but are intensely private? Just because it is the buzz and everyone is on that bandwagon, does it work for everyone? Or does everyone needs to take the time to understand how the latest buzz will, will not, or needs to be massaged, to work for them? Fads, trends, and new waves of thought often make me think of lemmings to the sea—everyone wildly runs towards the cause, without thinking of what is going on or where it will take us. We have accepted that terrible image as reality. It wasn't until recently that I learned lemmings don't tend to jump off cliffs into the ocean in mass suicides. Lemmings can swim, don't tend to run in a pack to their deaths, and have had a plan, albeit instinctual, which creates a new entity. Even the mindless lemming knows what it needs.

Level III: How Do I React to Authority?

Level III starts to get us where we live. Because we are the smart kids, the people who have the answers, and who are unwilling to admit that maybe they need a little help. In other words, how do we deal with other people in control? It's a big question because we all think we're easygoing and that we work well with each other, are team players, and part of the gang (even though we might think we are, or are with, the leaders and leadership part of the gang). In a coaching relationship, you're going to hear what you're missing; that's just the nature of the beast. It's what you signed up for.

The unofficial construct is that the coach has some great wisdom you can't seem to figure out. You consent to pay the coach an agreed-upon amount to help you figure out your wisdom. Help! In this construct, you will be challenged. You will be called out on your indiscretions, your failings, your areas of want. You will be asked what your real intentions are. And because this isn't a friend or family member, the punches won't be pulled. You will get asked real questions. It might not be comfortable. And you might not be comfortable. And you will not like it. Or parts of it. And you will not like some of your own answers. And you will not want to admit what some of your answers are.

It's important to know if you withdraw from confrontation, if you get combative when people fail to see your reply is the best one or they don't think you have the best thing since sliced bread, or if you typically withhold who you are to be likable or part of the crowd. If you check out from being who you are from fear of being disliked, then accept that this will not be your last coach, class, seminar, webinar, or retreat. You are not in the room. Your persona or aspirational self is in the room. Every coaching relationship involves accepting that we do not know as much as we think we do. That means abdicating being in control, being the expert, being the smart/talented /savvy one in the room.

When we are unable to accept that truth, we hijack our ability to fully take in the wisdom, knowledge, or talents we have said we want to obtain or the lessons from the very person we have asked to teach us. Everything we're doing personally, we're doing professionally, and it may or may not be what's holding us back. But our tendencies will most assuredly be made known in the process; sometimes the lesson will be easy and sometimes we will be kicking and screaming.

If you don't like being reminded of what you meant to do but haven't gotten to yet or have forgotten to do—from laundry to professional tasks — it is very probable you have a problem with authority or someone questioning you. You may have a defensiveness with which you have not yet come to terms.

How well do we finesse being called to be accountable?

How well do we finesse our darker, base, less altruistic emotions?

How comfortable are we with the duality of every nature, quality, experience?

And how well do we finesse allowing these thoughts and emotions being brought out into the open for discussion and analysis? After all, we thought this was going to be about achieving results and embracing our best self. What is this introspection stuff? We thought this was about answers, not questions.

Level IV: How Good Is My Time Management?

Level IV is a tough one. We all think that we are moving and shaking and getting a lot of things done every day. For the most part, that's very true, but it's also very true that sometimes adding one more task to the daily list can undo you.

Knowing how well you can bounce back is important. Knowing you are clear on what you can and cannot do is even more important. Knowing how much you can disrupt your daily schedule is vital because working with a coach is inconvenient. It means losing that hour of sleep. It means doing research and reading that isn't for your book club so you can't wing it or say you ran out of time. You're going to have to learn things, report on things, explain things, and be honest about how they fit into your life or not. And that is inconvenient.

The realities of working with a coach bring questions into any relationship, and we will be tested. Working with a coach may be perceived by a partner as being selfish. It may open up relationship problems that were under the surface. Things no one wanted to see for the very same reason—it takes time to acknowledge, time to work on them, time to fix them, time to heal. And none of us seems to have enough time.

It seems to me the notion of selfishness comes down to that very question—a question of time. Time management isn't just about the number of hours in the day, although it may be natural to think that at first. If it was just about clocking in from location to location, that would be easy. But in everyday life, there are the conversations, the emotions, the unexpected plans, the emotional financing of friends, family, and loved ones with moments of time from a finite daily clock. When you add an hour or two a day of additional commitments to an already busy schedule, time management is as much about the emotions and intellect as it is about the clock. We've all lost more time to our emotions or to the emotions of someone we care about than we care to admit. Yet we still think of time as a unit of measure, not a fluid experience defined by moments.

Level V: Is This What I Want or Is This My Distraction?

Level V will come out of level IV because we're starting to give up things and we're starting to have people be upset with us, annoyed with us, and we don't like it. We would all like change to happen during the television commercial break so that our day-to-day routine is uninterrupted—we just end up new and improved.

This is when we start to ask ourselves good questions. It's one thing to think it would be a pleasant idea to open a store. It's another thing entirely to have an all-consuming passion for being the owner of the premiere boutique for widgets on Rodeo Drive. The language alone tells you the difference. Is your attitude,

"This is something I thought would be fun to do" or is it, "This something I have to do"? Only you can answer that question.

Level V is when all the unresolved things will come creeping forward. Am I worthy of this success? Can I do this? Why would anyone believe I could be the one to make it happen? I've had good ideas, and some of them have been pretty good. Is this one of the superb ones?

When we're daydreaming and thinking escapist thoughts, everything's possible. We've had that pipe dream that surfaces around the barbecue, the conversation of what might be.

When it's the real deal, we don't know why we need to do it, but we need to do it. So many new things start to come up through our psyches. We still might be very scared. We still might not even know why we're scared. But we know if we don't do it, we will always regret it.

Conversely, we might want to talk about doing this item because everyone will approve it and it will keep us all occupied, and this is close to what I'd like to do, but I'm afraid of that big dream. I'm going to distract myself with a little dream that I feel is safe. Or distract myself with a million legitimate sounding things so that when I am unable to get to it, no one will think less of me.

Distractions can be many things and hide many emotions. Distractions, like justifications, help give us permission to not do it. They give a societally accepted excuse to avoid the dream or life not lived. They allow us to give plausible excuses to ourselves, our friends, our communities.

Coaches will ask you the questions you don't want to answer. They understand that dreams are as essential as breath and sleep, and a dream may sustain you and your soul more than food at times. A coach will know when you are all in, partially in, or in the dream and fantasy of distraction and escape.

33

Distractions are excuses. What's worse is that we know they are excuses. The reason we hold onto them so tightly and release them so slowly is that it is hard to be very brave, very raw, and very open, and say I am going to do this. No matter what. Whether I am a success or failure. I will do this for me. This is serious work now. Am I willing to be honest with myself so that I might be honest with my coach? Am I willing to be brave? "Brave" not in caveman terms of fighting the animal at the cave entrance, but am I willing to fight the internal jailor at my psyche's door? Do I have what it takes to embrace the experience, not success or failure, as my unique experience? Be willing to ride it to completion, and own it outside of the arbitrary markers of what is currently deemed success, rejection, or failure? Can I own my actions and own myself? Am I brave enough to not outrun the metaphorical beast with fangs but to look into the abyss of myself and accept what I see, know, and learn?

Level VI: What Is My Real Relationship with Money?

Money. Money. Money. Money. Money. Money. Money. Money. Makes the world go around. Makes life easier. [The love of] money is the root of all evil. Many qualities and traits are associated with money. The only one that counts is your relationship with it. There are people who have never known want, just as there are people who've never known plenty. Most of us fall in the middle.

How do you look at your finances? Are you comfortable investing in yourself? Do you feel you should be able to do it all on your own? If you have your answer, it will make it easier for you to work with someone. Because when you start working with a coach, there will be reading materials, research materials, improvements for your business, and other unexpected expenses.

Are you comfortable spending money on yourself? Most people would say no problem, but paying your utility bills is not spending money on yourself. It's addressing core needs.

How we approach money says a lot about how we value ourselves and how we were raised to value ourselves. It's not surprising that America has more financial hoarders than most other countries. People who are raised in what Americans might consider abject poverty, no matter how much money they acquire, never feel it is theirs or that it will last. They have lived a small life for so long, fearing one day they would not have enough for whatever comes down the road, that no matter how much they might acquire, the fear does not let them feel it is ever sufficient. More often than not, they leave enormous windfalls to strangers or institutions, not necessarily to family, because often the fear had compromised their life, and their strangeness alienated people. Even though the Great Depression touched parents and grandparents and for some even great-grandparents, that sense of lack has been shared with each subsequent generation.

It doesn't help that many of us have experienced the ever-changing economic tides of recessions, the great recession, and stock market debacles. We have known that feeling of scarceness or known someone else who has. It will surprise you how it trips you up.

If time management is a hard hurdle to jump over, money is the marathon. Our financial situations tend to be in a state of flux. More than that, a vast majority of the financial gurus advise saving, delaying, and caution with our money for the future. An approach to life that seems to have a finiteness rather than an option for consideration. That shows how little we understand the value and relationship we have with money individually, societally, or culturally. Even the soap operas and television shows focus us on the haves and the have-nots. It would seem to reinforce that sense of transitoriness money has. At any moment, it could all be gone.

But we don't think that way about chocolate. Or gas, oil, and fuel. Or food. Or a long list of items that we need and use on a daily basis. We have given filthy lucre a power not given to other commodities. And in some ways, we do lose our soul, our health to filthy lucre, because we become stuck in our personal, professional, social, educational, you-name-it lives, for we are apprehensive about the cost—financial and emotional—that change may bring about. Very rarely is change considered an improvement, enhancement, addition, or in a constructive light. Isn't that an interesting construct? We seem to suffer from cultural metathesiophobia, the fear of change.

Money becomes the socially acceptable way to stay stuck, to avoid change, to not alter your course, to follow the prudent course of action.

It is the easy answer to why you didn't, couldn't, think twice about it. When we don't understand family histories, boom-and-bust cycles, stories of every failure but never every success, fortune-smiled-upon-the-blessed-children views of our world, we cannot help but repeat, redo, revisit, and release the hopes we've had for our personal greatness. What is your relationship to money?

Level VII: Can I Accept the Responsibility for Changing My Life?

Level VII is the hardest of all. Because if we really believed everything we said we want and believe we should have, the world would be filled with healthy, slender, kind, empathetic, generous, entrepreneur millionaires. The fact that the world is not filled with healthy, slender, kind, empathetic, generous, entrepreneur millionaires—and I'm sure you have a few traits you would love to put in there as well—exemplifies the disconnect between what we say we want and what we achieve. Every Monday we might begin a new diet. Every January, health club memberships explode. Regretfully, America continues to be a land of weight, heft, and health issues. It's not that people don't want a healthy, slender body. It is just that our reality is determined by popcorn at the movies on a date and a glass of wine with girlfriends and a million other little surprises that we don't refuse.

I'm not advocating leaving the world to accomplish your dream. I am advocating knowing how to achieve your dream and taking responsibility for the path to get you there. Ultimately, it is always our choice. Knowing yourself will help you get there or at least help you understand if you don't choose to go there.

This is where the last devil waits for you. He is insidious and simple and honest and terrifying and within. He is fear. None of like to admit that we are or might be scared. That is something one leaves behind in childhood, long ago. We know the Wolfman isn't coming to the front door to scare us. We know if we study enough we can pass the test we need to graduate. We hope to find love and are afraid we might never marry, but we aren't in a state of fear that if that doesn't happen, terrible things will. We spend a lot of our life being comfortable. Okay. Isn't it interesting that when someone asks us how we are, we answer okay? Not great. Not fabulous. Okay. "Okay" is the dictum of our existence and being okay is okay with us.

Except it isn't. Whether you are looking for a coach to improve your bowling game, a coach to help your child study, a coach to assist you in business, a coach to help you process recent events in your life, a coach to help you move in your career or change your career, you are stating that you are *not* okay, and you want more. And this is good.

Okay exists to keep us all in check. Societally, we get nervous when someone goes off on a new tangent. That whole "the world isn't flat." Or gravity holds us to the earth. Or no person can run a five-minute or four-minute mile. These are ways we keep ourselves safe, and no one is challenged. The moment any of us want more, to not be merely okay, but to be good or great, we challenge the norm, the status quo. So it is not surprising that not only do friends and family try to protect us, but without knowing it, we try to protect ourselves. We do that through primal fear. That little voice that says this is okay. Don't go the extra step. No one needs that anyway. Who do you think you are? Smarter people would have already done this.

A million inner voices that harm us and hurt us and cry for us to stay where we are — these are simply fears trying to keep us safe, but instead, they harm us in so many different ways. Every so often, I think about what I have done in life and find for the most part that I don't think about what I have done, but what I didn't do. What I stopped myself from doing.

I was in Granada, Spain. In the caves of Sacromonte, being treated to a dance performance by the Gitanos, where my joy with their performance was apparent. At the end of one of the evenings, one of the most sensational dancers invited me, along with other audience members, to join in an impromptu dance at the end of the show. Our tour group had walked and hiked so much in those first few days of the trip that every part of me ached that night. I wasn't sure my knee would appreciate my challenging it to a new surprise. In my fear, I declined.

Here I am, years later, still regretting that I didn't throw caution to the wind and dance with the gypsies. Fear robbed me. I robbed myself. I take responsibility for my choice. It changed my life. It has made me want to never be in that position again, of not doing something I love for fear of a limitation I have mentally created. I am willing to take the responsibility for my choice. Fear allows us a rational, calm, reasonable way to not make our dreams come true. It isn't easy to say "this is mine." This is my responsibility; to accept my choices and decisions.

It makes me think of the person who wanted to sue McDonald's for making them fat. It wasn't McDonald's. It was the individual's choices and consumption, but we would all prefer to have someone to blame for why we did or did not do as we thought we would. Owning one's life is hard. It dares you to accept all of yourself, warts and all, and see what you want to keep and what you want to change. It is no small step to accept the challenge of responsibility.

When we seek outside help, we are separating from our people, and that is scary. We are, in many ways, stepping into the great unknown. Starting a business, going to college, placing your painting or prize muffins into a competition is scary. But each of those has actions has placed you beyond the limits of your fear, and you have both changed and grown. In some ways, I am thrilled to know there is no time limit on growth. To me, that means that up until my last breath, I can be looking at the world in new fantastic ways that might scare me. I am willing, sometimes reluctantly, sometimes readily, to accept the responsibility of being me, hopefully in my best version. That will mean accepting who *me* is.

Tests

Tests. Lots of tests. No, not those terrifying will-I-make-it, did-I-study-enough, my-life-depends-on-this tests. These are the fun ones we take ourselves. What kind of dog are you? What car are you? What what are you? You have seen them on Facebook forever. Before that, they emailed questionnaires that added up the points and told us who and what we were. It seems everyone is trying to wrangle you into one, sharing their new discoveries. These recent fun tests come from our desire, natural desire, to categorize. To know ourselves. To know others. Sometimes it is so we can better communicate and sometimes it is to gain an advantage, but either way, these tests do serve a purpose. They help us establish a sense of self, at times, looking at what we don't want to see, sometimes revealing traits and tendencies of which we are unaware. But all the same, they add to our sense of self and are great tools.

When I was serving on a nonprofit board, I received a questionnaire in the mail. Please fill this out, and we will discuss the results at the board retreat. Dutifully, I filled in my answers and was curious about where this journey would be taking me. A few weeks later, a brightly colored envelope arrived with my Birkman assessment. It was my first personality test. It didn't tell me anything I didn't already have a sense of, for the most part, only confirming what I thought. I'm verbal and, no surprise, I registered green and blue. But I did learn about the other colors—the red and yellow people—and how their approach to the world could be so very different from mine. And how my efforts to be so helpful might just be entirely misunderstood, time-consuming, and even annoying. We see things that differently. I am not making light of an extensive, well thought out, well-respected system of understanding. For many people, it was eye-opening. It was for me. Another long-standing type indicator is the Myers-Briggs assessment. This is also a system with decades of use and understanding. It has found favor once again, and people couldn't believe I hadn't had my MBTI (Myers-Briggs Type Indicator) determined. A friend who knows me very well and who has done the analysis for many offered to do mine. What was most interesting is she saw me as an extrovert, where I see myself more as an introvert. Again, valuable information for me. I may feel one way but present another. Was she wrong? No. That is how I present. Am I wrong? I don't believe so. And the other truth is that, at all times, we are evolving and changing. I may very well have been more of an extrovert but am becoming more introverted. Or vice versa.

Through the years, tests have become more different, humorous, silly, and fun, and yet we continue to take them. We seek knowledge, and self-knowledge at that. Eneagrams are currently all the rage. Are they bad? Are they good? They are simply tools to better understand one's self in the world about them. No, I have not yet done one. Would I like to? Of course. I am on my own journey, my own quest. Why wouldn't I want to hear the tales of others as I go forth? Why wouldn't I want to learn of a new path and where it might take me? Why wouldn't I open myself to the possible?

Why mention these tests? Why mention works I like? I have often discovered things because someone mentioned them to me. It becomes a surprise gift when someone recommends an author and tells me why. Some of these suggestions I didn't care for; some captured me in ways I never would have expected. I have found myself with tears coming down my face because something so resonated with me that my soul cried out and would not be denied. I have read other books or taken a test that did not ring true to me or for me — for whatever reason — as well.

Here are a few of the self-awareness, self-assessment tests for your consideration. I am not endorsing any of these, nor are they the only tests available.

Each test focuses on the same, yet remarkably different, traits and patterns. There are similarities, but the nuance of the answer is often a differentiating factor.

Enneagrams

Thanks to the ancients, enneagrams have been part of our collective consciousness almost from the start of recorded time. However, like almost everything else, this concept has many parents, and many claim to be the "father" of this now modern and relevant approach to knowing one's tendencies and traits. Relying on archetypal characteristics, there are nine classifications with subcategories to fully flesh out each description.

Enneagrams have found renewed relevance in business life and have always been a consideration in spiritual development. They have had a recent resurgence in the consciousness of thought and business leaders.

Birkman

Roger Birkman developed his own system to understand communication and interaction — the Birkman Method. Birkman's experiences with pilot performance led him into the field of psychology. Looking at the misinterpretations and inaccurate perceptions encompassing personal, interpersonal, visual, and interactive incidents in action, led him to the study that would define him. Patterns, perceptions, influences, motivation, and behaviors combined to form his four primary categories that relate to how each of us processes and interprets. Perspective. Of course, once you are aware of your Birkman classification, you will be both surprised and reassured because everything seems to "make sense." To colorfully make sense.

Myers-Briggs

All it takes is the ability to see patterns, and that is exactly what Myers-Briggs is all about. Myers-Briggs combines the theory of Carl Jung's work into systems and categories. Traits are identified to facilitate one's understanding about how she or he processes information, in order to better understand how others process the same information given their filters and perceptions. Looking at the duality of traits—the yin and the yang—one's own tendencies become defined and categorized. The darling of the workplace, Myers-Briggs created an easily identifiable shorthand for personnel in human resources and other departments to discuss new hires.

The Keirsey Temperament Sorter

David Keirsey's book, *Please Understand Me,* examines issues of style and communication. Using a system based on four focused components, he found classifications to assist us in understanding one another, and more importantly, understanding our own way of communicating. Keirsey's work covers private, professional, and social worlds, focusing on the whole person and personality in all aspects of life. This includes the duality of each action, the strength and lack, failings and success. He also looks at the distinct aspect of what we say and what we do, and how those two dimensions of human behavior affect everything in our lives.

16 Personalities

Based on Jungian philosophy, this test also looks at the duality of nature and the internal versus the external world. Looking at how and where one's energy is derived shifts the idea of introversion as shyness or extroverts as being socially adept. Seeing the individual in layers of energy, filters, and categories allows for more in-depth analysis of the person and personality.

Personality Tests

One of the joys of the Internet is that we can take a test today to determine our hair color type, what kind of dog we might be, where we should vacation, and more, much more. (With all Internet offerings, and particularly with free tests online, please be aware that some are genuine sites offering self-help and knowledge, and others may be collecting your information for marketing purposes.)

Each test offers a chance for fun. Each test provides a degree of insight. Each test asks you a question, and whether you agree or disagree with the results, sometimes realizing you like the mountains more than the beach can give you an insight you didn't have before, or help explain why that college trip to the Jersey Shore was such a disappointment.

Paying attention to your responses as you answer any quiz helps you understand more of who you are and your preferences. I am a cheeseburger girl. That doesn't mean I don't like a good steak or that I would say no to lobster. It means that, when I'm asked my favorite food, I remember my childhood and barbeques in the backyard with friends and family. I recall summers of swimming until dinner was called, grabbing a burger, and jumping back in the pool. Yes, I do like a good cheeseburger, but—more than the food itself—the mental and memory connections make it my favorite. Does this mean I am not chic because I didn't say caviar and champagne? I believe it makes me real and honest with myself. I can also wax poetic on the virtues of a good grilled cheese sandwich. My favorite food is based on memory more than gustatory sensation.

The truer we are to ourselves and our whole selves, the clearer we are about who we are, the clearer we can be on what we need and where we want to go. Consider it your preparation and homework before finding your coach. Do you need to do it? No. You can do anything you want. It is your journey. But I wouldn't set out on a trip without packing; some might say over-packing, all that I believe I will need. We take bottled water when we get in the car to go to dinner, where it is a safe assumption they will have water. We take a sweater, jacket, or coat when we hear there is a chance of rain. We buy extra rolls for our big dinner party or another event. That said, yes, there are still people who like to wing it, and you very well might be one. So listen to yourself; you already know much about yourself and how you process. And that is what this is all about. Knowing what you need, knowing how we sabotage, knowing what we hope, knowing what we fear, and going forward anyway.

PART II
THEM

Knowing yourself is the beginning of all wisdom.

—ARISTOTLE

Coaching 101

Who's your coach?

In the beginning, there was Mom. My mom had all the answers, even if I rolled my eyes at half of them. As I got older, there were grandmothers, my godmother, even treasured friends of the family, and they had another batch of answers. As I got older still, I braved asking my father, for I knew he knew things as well, although the lessons often came at a cost.

The world was simpler then, or simpler than it seems now. As I became a young adult, I discovered that while my elder generation knew much, they were, in my opinion, still limited. They had not availed themselves of the new things. They did not think about the bigger questions of life, or if they did, I never heard an utterance about it. Like every teenager, I knew I knew it all. Those older people were fools!

Of course, with time it became apparent they were much savvier than I gave them credit for, but that is why they say youth is wasted on the young. Time marches on. I felt I was fortunate that along the road of life, a variety of other experts began to develop new ways of thinking. I had the luxury of education to wander about and with the advent of "leisure time" and intellectual pursuits, I began to explore new philosophies, religions, and approaches to life. The world changed. My world changed.

How?

As I wandered down the roads of thought, I developed a sort of roadmap or at least a roadmap from my perspective. So much of this is from my point of view, now with a few years traveling along. That has given me the necessary distance to see how I, like so many others, have lost the "me" in my hopes, and how I have lost trust in my opinions and thoughts.

When people were struggling to get food on the table and a place to sleep, it was difficult to look at the conceptual "bigger" ideas. The changes people have experienced in the last five hundred years are remarkable. Life experience was once limited to the essentials: growing and harvesting food, getting a meal, obtaining or constructing a place to be away from the elements, having a safe place to sleep. Life had immediate consequences if basic needs were not met. Without shelter, people died from exposure. Without maintaining crops, finding food could be difficult. Livestock was a luxury that needed care and feeding. Finding time to think, to look for answers to improve the human condition, was difficult.

There is a reason the Renaissance was so significant. Education and thought expanded. With that, the newly affluent began to offer patronage of the arts to establish themselves as people of value and culture. With the Industrial Revolution, machines and later technology began to replace human labor and could do the jobs of many. Not being in the field from morning to night allowed people time to think, to become educated, to read more than the Bible or religious texts or poetry. There was time to not only think, but to question, and with the questions, began the schools of thought that have revolutionized our worlds. Or so it seems to me. I present my view of how we have shifted our thoughts and taken in the wisdom of others for consideration.

Starting in the 1880s, Germans Nietzsche, Kant, and Kierkegaard, and the British Kant and Hegel, and Americans Ralph Waldo Emerson and Henry David Thoreau explored and expounded new philosophies. *Science and Health with Key to the Scriptures* by Mary Baker Eddy was indeed revolutionary. Humankind's relationship to nature and our disconnect from all that was safe and known were questioned at the time of the Industrial Revolution. The Virgin and the Dynamo. Nature displace by mechanization. Now throw in the theories of Sigmund Freud, Alfred Adler, and Carl Jung, and suddenly everything was open for interpretation and questioning. Not only was the world in an uproar, socially, politically, and culturally, but we were in our own uproar.

In this age of intellectual pursuit, tinkering, creating, inventing, removing limits from the workplace, and fueling the perception of social mobility, all was open for review. But then British chemist Sir William Crookes uttered a startling line in 1898 that launched a world of unintended consequences: "England and all civilized nations stand in deadly peril." He predicted global famine and questioned the future of humankind, but advocated adding nitrogen to soil to improve food production. Thomas Hager's *The Alchemy of Air* explores the work of Fritz Haber and Carl Bosch as they developed that process to make nitrogen fertilizer. However, the Haber-Bosch process could also be used to make explosives and the process was used with devastating effect in World War I and II.

The book is an eye-opener to the utopian hope of egalitarianism, social mobility, the breakdown of religious barriers, the merit of one's work, and intellectual abilities that are sadly dashed—to say nothing of the law of unintended consequences. But it speaks to the attitude of "anything is possible"—an attitude that was widespread as the Victorian empire expanded in land mass and influence, and German nationalism rose as principalities became states.

In the twentieth century and across the pond—here in America—our thinkers launched their philosophies. Henry Ford revolutionized the workplace. Dale Carnegie explained *How* to *Win Friends and Influence People* and Napoleon Hill told Americans to *Think and Grow Rich.*

WWI brought tragedy but also innovation and the training of many doctors. Penicillin revolutionized the treatment of illness. The doctor could keep death at bay with the right knowledge and health care, and science continued to expand. Even the Wall Street crash didn't quite do us in, although it limited access to everything but thought.

When we hit the 1940s, the exaltation of science reached a dizzying height in WWII, enough to scare us into reviewing where we were and where we were going. Mostly we wanted a kinder, easier world. But the genie was out of the bottle and with it came a host of new questions. And with questions, post-WWII America found a variety of new experts.

Our newfound medical experts, like Dr. Spock, explained to us the wisdom that we previously would have sought from the collective wisdom.

New brides of war heroes weren't living near family or friends, but in new communities far away; their husbands were taking advantage of the GI Bill and they were pursuing the American Dream. By the 1950s, it could be said that in some ways, affluence and the "good life" was even harder to live with than austerity and the threat and fears of wartime.

The late comedian George Carlin accurately called it when he spoke of the euphemisms for war trauma. What was called in World War I "shell shock"—with an immediacy in the words—became less clear with each new definition. And each new definition lessened the emphasis on personal trauma. In World War II, the term became "battle fatigue" and later "post-traumatic stress disorder."

As the questions of life got more involved, we delved deeply and went for psychoanalysis. "My years on the couch" implied education and affluence. We stopped going to past generations for knowledge within their sphere of influence, and sought wisdom instead from books and newly labeled experts and theorists.

Synanon, Alcoholics Anonymous, Weight Watchers. It seemed there was a group with an answer to every problem. We knew it. We could get answers from the unique collective.

It marked an interesting shift from self-discovery to the notion of being flawed or broken and in need of a fix. A fascinating and subtle change. Because when we are broken, we need professionals to fix us. And isn't it interesting that the breakdown in trust, of questioning authority, and all the beginnings of tumultuous times coincide with the belief we are broken? The questions are even more fascinating, but we don't trust ourselves to answer them.

The floodgates opened. Now it wasn't experts but theories and schools of thought. Let's hear it for Flower Power. Age of Aquarius. What's your sign? Are we compatible? Our distrust of everything that might have any taint of authority or credence took us to touchy-feely hoodoo voodoo. We not only liked it, we thrived on it. The religious backlash manifested in evangelical, back-to-basics, and charismatic leaders. How was Charles Manson's "family" acceptable? The Church of Bible Understanding (formerly known as the Forever Family)? The People's Temple and Jim Jones? The Unification Church and Reverend Sun Myung Moon? The Twelve Tribes and Elbert Eugene Spriggs? Children of God/The Family of Love/The Family? Our social unrest and injustice moved in two different directions. Symbionese Liberation Army. The Black Panthers. Students for Democratic Society. Not only did we reject traditional wisdom and traditional values, we no longer trusted traditional institutions. But that much rejection always swings back the other direction just as easily and often all too quickly.

So it's no surprise that we started to discover therapy, counseling, Rolfing, EST, and a host of other philosophies to answer the burning questions in our souls. Therapists, psychologists, and psychiatrists once again held court on the questions of our lives. And it was comforting. So were evangelical faiths. Being born again became chic. Going to the Bible for counseling was all the rage. A wild embrace of all that was traditional and strangely comforting, limiting and familiar, and none of it requiring thought or work. Or the absolute opposite direction with intense delving into one's core. Lifespring and other New Age human-potential groups gained ground. More interestingly, the pursuit of financial gain developed religious-like status and we entered the age of conspicuous over-consumption. This was reflected in TV shows such as *Family Ties, Dallas,* and *Dynasty,* and the film *Wall Street.* In *Wall Street,* the character Gordon Gekko extolled the virtue of greed without regret, remorse, or emotion. To say nothing of the self-medication and rise of pharmacology—freelance and professional—of which we availed ourselves. We felt guilty but looked good while we found people to give us the answers we wanted.

But change is the only constant, and whether you believed in these movements and theories or not, a lot of people did. Welcome to the time of Soothsayers, Ramtha, Lazarus, Voices of the Elders, inhabiting current bodies. There has always been the ever-ongoing collection of religious, scientific or cult-like programs with which people have become infatuated. In fairness, many people benefited. Most did not. But it speaks to our search for answers and understanding. New Age was our age, and going in was all the rage.

As we became more educated, not only with degrees but with computers and programs, with travel and other cultures, in languages—foreign or mechanical—we became more comfortable with being categorized and specialized. If we could get a handle on someone, we could know their type and work them for our needs. We might have said the goal was to understand them, but the subtext was always to help us facilitate bringing our desires to fruition. If there was a test, we could take it, and it would give us our answers. Be it through Myers-Briggs, Birkman, the four agreements, or any of the wonderful, interesting books we read, we could find a benchmark of success or learn how to strive to the next place. People announced themselves as an ENFP, an ISFJ. Were you a blue? Did you process as a red, or did you run a spectrum into yellow? Counseling, therapy, analysis—we did them. We learned from them. We reveled in self-discovery. We reveled in understanding others. We reveled in a period of over-disclosure, with every family secret becoming public and processed, not in our private lives or local community, but in the public arena. Think Phil—Donahue or McGraw. Oprah. Sally Jesse Raphael. Geraldo. It feels daunting that the private confessional became a televised show on a topic of the day/week/moment/month/year. Cocktail parties were full of secrets, stories, and problem-solving. After all, we were now becoming experts, too. Until a subtle presence crept into our lives, or perhaps I should say something crept out of our lives. Something important. Privacy.

2000s

When everyone has an "issue," people get nervous. Laws change. Society circles the wagons. Employers get edgy. But twenty years earlier, business had not become so focused on profitability, and—some might say—just plain, cold, hard bottom lines. By the 2000s, human resource departments had twenty years of the new world and working with everyone's "needs," and it was exhausting, costly, and tedious. It is tiring being understanding. Any of us with a friend losing the same ten pounds knows that. The new approach was to ward off problems before they became problems.

Suddenly, seeing a psychiatrist, psychologist, or other counselor became an albatross. It was in your health history. Employers could ask you about your mental health, and if you had a history, you might not have a future. Worrying about weight in the age of over-disclosure became as dangerous as psychosis. They might not have known if your Prozac was prescribed for depression or weight loss, but if you had Prozac in your medical history, you could be deemed suspect. Seeking professional help via the traditional method was now something that could hurt you. Medical files, employment history, even credit history became part of job applications. Just as business circled the wagons, so did John Q. Public.

We are natural seekers. We want knowledge. Experience. Validation. Security. Supporters. Advice.

One could even argue as the world got quicker, faster, we no longer wanted to put in the time to do the serious interior work or even take the full responsibility for a poor decision.

Dr. Phil comes to mind. Suddenly we had a no-nonsense, tell-it-like-it-is, commonsense, here's-what-you-do approach to the problems of life. And it felt good. And easy. And tempting.

Now add the fact that we like our sports with their clearly defined rules and lines. Marry the two, and suddenly a spiritual guide previously only available to the very few becomes accessible to many.

Welcome to the time of coaches. This new place to go is a variation on all of the above. All the decades' trends, knowledge, and wisdom. It combines the best of the interpersonal with the joys of technology; it's charming with the cult of possibility and personality, all the while encouraging you to be your best self.

Life coach. Style coach. Business coach. Coach.

The word is no longer for sports alone. The word "coach" has more meanings and followers than those five letters ever had before. Or ever imagined possible.

In our complicated world, the idea of someone to help us navigate the roadmap of confusion is a desirable thought. In an age that outsources everything—from what to wear to grocery shopping to meal delivery to aspects of our work to childcare to test preparation to health care advocates—here is another way to make the work of living, the choices of life, easier and less demanding. We have enough to address. Better yet, there are many fabulous people out there who honestly just want to share their knowledge, their wisdom, their discoveries. This is by no means a putdown of anyone else.

There is a reason why the "Dummies" book series has done so well. With too many demands on our time and without much free time, we all want to have someone quickly help us find the best use of our time.

That is what this book is intended for as well. For you to be able to ask the question and get the answer you didn't know you needed.

As I have said for a long time, "Please allow my expensive therapy to pay off for you." As my father used to say, I'm kidding on the square. The truth is I have spent a good amount of money searching for answers. Primarily in traditional ways, but I've also belonged to a variety of organizations that have valued developing the individual, and so I benefited by personality and leadership skill assessments.

Even though I knew my Myers-Briggs, my Birkman, my you-fill-in-the-blank results, when I started working with coaching professionals, I had no idea how clueless I was as to what I was looking for or trying to find. It is hard to get an answer if you do not know your question.

As I look at navigating the world of coaches, I see that very much is right. I believe I've been very fortunate in the people I've encountered. I've heard stories of others who haven't been as fortunate. No desire to bash them or the professionals with whom they worked. This is to help you decide what will work for you. What is your real need? And, realistically, how much time do you have available? What is your financial comfort level? That topic comes along at the end of every sales pitch.

So let's work on empowering ourselves to the best experience possible the next time you see that seminar, webinar, teleconference, skills assessment, online class, Skype classroom, lifestyle adventure, you name it, another "growth opportunity."

Let's get to *Finding Your Coach*.

Know Thy Teacher! Know Thyself!

Many years ago, I was undergoing personal difficulties. It was the 1980s. I was a child of the times, and so, of course, the situation called for a mental health professional. I had no idea the alphabet soup into which I was about to dive. I thought they were all doctors until I learned only the psychiatrists were doctors.

What about the psychologists? Who would politely explain the difference in their choice to practice as they had?

There were licensed clinical social workers—a whole other alphabet soup that also offered answers depending on the need.

Add to that the marriage and family counseling specifications, adolescent counseling, and then as time went on, the start of the niche therapists and specific need programs.

From coping with your mother to coping with behaviors to coping with addictions to coping with whatever lemons life has given you, there would be someone for you.

I worked with an LCSW, puzzling away at my questions and demons. Ultimately, success or failure of that collaboration is mine. The integrity of the process and information was always coming from me to them. I did not know or realize what my real questions were. I was distracted by the cacophony of elements in my life that kept me busy and occupied but not necessarily looking at or doing the work for change and growth.

That's not to say that I didn't experience change and growth. It's a rare squirrel that doesn't find chestnuts on the ground. But when I reflect on that time, there were many other doors I could have opened. I may not have made different choices, but the decisions I made might have come from a larger understanding.

I suppose one could say the rise of the self-help movement occurred in the decade of the '80s. John Bradshaw, Louise Hay, Carolyn Myst, Naomi Wolf, Geneen Roth, Leo Pascalia—the world was suddenly filled with intelligent, thoughtful people looking at our past, our present, our history, and affecting our futures. We loved it. We reveled in it. With a few books, we were brilliant.

Or at least I thought I was becoming so.

Therapy

The day I started paying someone for answers about the secrets of my soul, an entirely different expectation was created. A wide variety of professionals is available to help us with this: psychiatrist, psychologist, licensed clinical social worker, marriage and family counseling, 12-step program leader, paid group facilitator. Each of these people brought something to the mix.

There's individual therapy or one-on-one, where we went into the details of wrongs perceived and rights hoped for, and we combined obscuring the truth with seeking it. Open books are never all that open. There's delusion and a degree of withholding—intentional or otherwise.

Self-preservation goes on in the room. It takes a very brave person to be totally raw, bare, and vulnerable in the therapy setting. Group therapy gave us the opportunity to see lots of other "crazy" people. They were just as crazy as we were. It was comforting and scary. At their best, brave souls shared their battles to help others to find the tools to fight their fights.

Lin Schussler-Williams says the difference between therapy and coaching is one looks at the past and the other looks toward the future. I think that's a very apt remark. I also believe that it takes a significant degree of self-awareness to be searching and seeking, and without looking at one's past, it may be hard to move into the future.

Why mention this?

Because your self-knowledge is going to help you with every interaction with every coach and with every program you select. Even if you're working with someone on purely business issues at some point, the unruly five-year-old within you will rise and sabotage some moment in your program. Knowing who your inner five-year-old is will allow you to move forward, smile, and break through your limitations.

The Search

I believe we are all lifelong seekers. Truth. Wisdom. A real bargain with bragging rights. We can use those talents to find help for ourselves.

How do we find a coach? How do we trust some odd stranger to be an agent of change? How do we risk with confidence if we have a limited amount of trust and hope? The fear and apprehension we feel limit us. That, in turn, tends to limit our results. We hold back instead of embracing what could happen or might change. How do we find the miracle, the exception, the source of bragging rights in our future? We search.

And it has never been easier, which ironically, can make things harder, too. The advantage of the traditional outlets of the medical field is there is an accountability factor that gives us some peace of mind. Licensing. Education requirements. Hours of practice, service, clinical work. Perhaps it is a false peace of mind, but there is the "adult supervision" aspect that makes us feel better. Safer. Protected. A hierarchy of who can do what based on letters from MD to LCSW to MFCC and a few in between.

I present the following story not to terrify you, but to help you listen to your inner voice. To help you know that there are a lot of great people with a bad website and a lot of great sites with a broad range of talents behind the click.

I knew an individual who had an ongoing mental health issue. Rather than seek further or additional medical attention, perhaps from fear or maybe not understanding what was happening internally, this person began to explore other options.

In the search, this person found an energy worker/healer/coach. Soon enough, the feelings were those of amazement and wonder at this life coach's knowledge and insights, and with his support and encouragement, the individual felt healed. With an equilibrium perceived to be once again balanced, the announcement came forth that a new career choice had been decided, and a life and business as a life coach were starting.

With much energy and enthusiasm, this person approached the new profession as one might start a Fortune 500 company, with the hiring of an assistant, creation of a branded logo and identity, color concept consultation, elegant stationery and letterhead, business cards and flyers. For the website, a professional photographer was hired. For the photo shoot, a makeup artist and stylist were brought in, with wardrobe consultations, as well. The site was designed and had elegant (for the time) technologies, including audio playbacks, recorded information sessions, and audio segments on topics.

A blog featured weekly updates on themes and issues. The posts were interesting, timely. They raised interesting questions and sounded personal and compelling. Professional pages and information was immediately listed on Facebook and LinkedIn. The individual and the assistant canvassed the neighborhood for clients.

From the website and description, the person presented seemed competent, educated, and someone worth contacting for a complimentary session. This is from the Google profile page created from the website (edited to anonymize).

Story Introduction

X is a spiritual life coach helping people to realize the power they hold in their thoughts, choices, and beliefs … Once a champion athlete in [sport], playing with the greats like [Big Player] and [Famous Player], X is now a writer and life coach. [A] current novel … is under consideration for publication. The philosophy behind the title is that all humans are beautiful [creatures] going through the world. X has traveled through Europe [solo] many times and has learned about physical travel but more importantly … has learned about the marathon of psychological, emotional, and spiritual journey. As X says, "There is Power in Knowledge, but there is, even more Power in Believing." XXXX Life Coach. Spiritual Life Coach/Empowering people through taking control of their thoughts and beliefs, present.

I look at this today and think even still, this sounds like someone I would be interested in consulting. It sounds and looks great, compelling, welcoming. Only I am aware this individual was in a full manic episode prior to a mental health break. Only I know the novel had been mailed to publishers, but had not received any interest or options at the time, nor since then. Only I know that in less than one year from this site going up, the person had left the area, left the practice that never took off in spite of hiring an assistant and office space, and the phone number was disconnected.

Now I have terrified you. That was not my intent. My intent is to point out that, in the wild, wild west of unregulated, well-intentioned, competent, capable, intelligent, helpful, and helping people and professionals, we all need to do our homework. We need to listen to our inner voice, ask questions of them and ourselves repeatedly.

My intent is to point out that the old tried-and-true ways of research still have merit. Just as you would look for a doctor, you might want to do the same here. Ask your friends, your colleagues, and your professional associations if they are familiar with coaches, coaching, and coaching programs. You will get an immediate reaction—positive or negative—and from there, you will know how to value their information.

You can go online and type in "coach" or "life coach," and you will be astonished at how many options pop up before your very eyes. This is just for the programs, certifications, and other possibilities. This isn't even for names of individuals who are coaching or taking clients. I am telling you this to give you some peace of mind, rather than to rattle you.

John F. Kennedy Jr. graduated from a prestigious university and law school. There was never a question as to his intelligence, his ability, or the quality of his education. He did not pass the bar on the first try. Others, from less well-known universities and law schools, did. We all come into our own at different times, bring different questions to the table, and sometimes process questions differently. He did pass, did practice, and did ultimately follow other passions until his untimely passing. All done in his own time.

One of the sharpest legal minds I know in his specialty had to make a harsh choice when he graduated from college decades ago. He knew he wanted to go into law. He knew that in the city in which he lived there were prestigious schools that would look impressive on a diploma on his wall. He knew what his time and financial considerations and constraints were. Ultimately, he chose a law school that suited his fiscal and other needs while providing excellent legal training, and which was later was absorbed into a larger, more prestigious law school. But this school, at the time, did not have the name factor of the other, more well-known schools. He kept his eye on the prize. Once he passed the bar, all that ultimately was important were the JD letters following his name.

Currently, he is a thriving Beverly Hills attorney in a land known for the sharks and brilliant legal minds and maneuvers. The moral of the tale is that, in knowing what he brought to the table, he realized he needed first to get to the table. Once there, he could stand on his talent and merits, and command what he wanted.

My experiences finding people have been mostly serendipitous. But I do have tales of other experiences, too, I regret to say. One of my first efforts was with an individual who worked through an organized, ongoing adult education, life enrichment center. I had recently returned to my university, where I had finished my last remaining classes to receive my degree. I was filled with boundless enthusiasm and belief as I embarked upon my new road.

While the credentials of the instructor seemed worthy of my trust, I quickly learned that we were not a good fit. After the fourth week of my ten-week course, I stopped going. For whatever reason, with me, the teacher's approach was to destroy, denigrate, or damn whatever I wrote, even when I rewrote it exactly to the specifications and recommendations she had made the week before. I don't know why we did not mesh, but we simply did not. Other people in the class validated the oddness of my experience with her. Perhaps in a past life, I stepped on her toe or stole her husband, but whatever I did, it appears to have had a significant half-life. What I did not realize was how off-putting it was for me and how it damaged my trust and confidence in working with other professionals.

Time passes. Things change. Things remain the same. Dreams, hopes, and goals creep back to the forefront of your mind. As we have all heard through the years, "When the student is ready, the master will appear."

I did my interpersonal work. I read my assortment of timely self-help books. I watched all the shows my peers and contemporaries watched. One day a friend I know, love, and respect (and who did my Myers-Briggs assessment), mentioned someone she had been working with; I was interested. I spoke with this new person. I liked what I was hearing. And I signed on. It wasn't until much later that I learned that not only is she certified through a respected thought leader, but she also has extensive education, including degrees in theology and religions, in addition to significant professional experiences and a career. I began to work with her, and even though I thought I was ready to go, progress wasn't instantaneous, quick, or easy. Perhaps for some others, but it appears that in my journey, I tend to hold myself back. I am speaking from an understanding that we dream big, but fear our dreams, too.

From that first contact came another. Again, someone had recommended her, and I met her at a retreat and had a follow-up conversation; it appeared her expertise would facilitate the next step in my progression and metamorphosis. And once again, little did I know, she had extensive credentials, certifications, books, clients, and contacts. The next referral came from a friend of mine who knew a particular thought leader through her journey and incarnations. I was introduced to her by my friend who took me as her guest to a nearby conference. I was intrigued, educated, challenged, and joined this group, this tribe. Through this new thought leader, life coach, and author, I have been exposed to many of her contemporaries in her field. These are people on the airwaves and in print, who are respected, and who share possibilities and projects with me.

Have I been lucky? Possibly. Do I trust my friends? Definitely. Am I that same neophyte to the learning game? Most certainly not. The secret is knowing that all kinds of instructors and coaches are out there—from the phenomenal to those who will be the source of the most outrageous story you'll be telling. Listen to your inner voice. Question. Trust. And do it all over again.

I love Sherlock Holmes and his logical, empirical mind, that clever deduce-it-all, rigid, finite, simple world that the stories of this character conjure up. I am sure he would be horrified by my touchy-feely suggestions. But I do believe that it is the combination of the two—the "trust, but verify" approach—that will help you find who you need.

The first time I learned about an online class, I thought it was the greatest thing since sliced bread. Granted, that was a long time ago, longer than I care to admit. The technology was primitive at best and the material dry. But at the time, it seemed preferable to listening to a dismal, opinionated, judgmental professor who pontificated rather than educated. However, what I did not know at that time is that my attention span, or perhaps my attention span to something dry and uninteresting, was very limited, and I could sign up, but completing was not my forte.

I did not know myself.

Even to this day, when I am in an all-day or all-morning or afternoon or evening conference, I am aware of my "doze off" moment. It has nothing to do with sleepiness, but rather I've hit my limit of monotone, monotony, and lack of movement. That is me knowing myself, and to any speaker who has thought they were losing me, I apologize. You were, but I was fighting it. Even with knowing this, there are programs and events I will and must attend. Knowing oneself is the difference in gleaning all the pearls of wisdom out there, or being able to say you took the class. The difference is tremendous.

So what are the new ways to receive your education, your coaching, your gleaning of pearls of wisdom? The ones I have noticed are the following:

- One-day seminars
- Weekend retreats
- Online programs with phone-in capabilities
- Teleconferences
- Webinars
- Skype appointments
- Groups
- One-on-one
- More are probably coming about as I type.

They are all good. They all offer something of merit. Knowing what your comfort level is and how you best receive and process information will be invaluable to you as you navigate these new waters.

Let's start with the easiest and most familiar: one-on-one.

One-on-One

One-on-one is the form of coaching I tend to think of when it comes to individual sports or endeavors. It is the form of coaching most people tend to think of when it comes to therapy. The one-on-one format is familiar from a guidance counselor, childhood mentor, or family friend, or from business or personal coaching. It is the most intimate and vulnerable method, as you share your hopes and dreams. You have retained someone to help you determine your path or point things out to you that you may have not realized will help you advance your dreams. Often we aren't thrilled to hear what is missing, but would prefer to hear how well we are doing.

Easy? Right?

We all know the answer to that is that it isn't easy. We tend to have great dreams that we *say* we want to achieve, but somehow when the alarm goes off in the morning, we don't rise to its call.

"I want to run a marathon, but I don't have the time to train."

"I want to play the guitar, but I can never find the time to practice."

"I'd love to be a gourmet chef, but I only cook for myself."

And the mantra of every January 1, or perhaps January 2, after the big celebrations: "I want to lose weight and get in great shape, but my day is so full already."

Do your interpersonal homework. It is very hard to become a public figure if you are a private person. It is very hard to be a great athlete if you doubt your ability to perform. It is hard to be a great dancer if you do not trust your partner will be there to catch you or cover your move.

You've probably noticed that if you have issues in these areas, you very well may have these same issues for and in your life and relationships. We have the same tendencies whether they are personal or professional. Is it criticism that gets under your skin, whether actual or perceived? The defensiveness or hurt feelings too often shut down the ability to hear what is really being said. The points being offered might help, but when we shut down, good advice gets lost.

In every coaching dynamic, there is the duality of issues at all times. Your coach wants you to succeed, sometimes more than you do. Your coach can only work with what you tell them and share with them, and the accuracy in what you are doing and sharing helps them to help you.

I have great respect for everyone I have encountered in the support realm. They have listened to my dreams. They have held my hopes. They have reminded me of my aspirations. And they have believed in me perhaps more than I did myself. They believed in my hope. They accepted or understood or saw that while the world was before me and all I had to do was take that one step, something within me was not allowing me to go forward. And yet they still believed. And they still hoped. And they still helped.

One-on-one will be the most direct, most immediate form of coaching. You cannot hide your facial expressions or your pause on the phone. Do you need to be accountable to someone? Do you need that parent or teacher to review your assignments? Do you need a weekly check-in to retool or refine your course? Do you need it weekly? Biweekly? Monthly?

One-on-one work isn't therapy, although there may be moments it feels that way. You may be working on your dream or dream project, but the learning that goes along with it is all about yourself, about how you react and how you respond.

This may be a form of coaching you need at the beginning, middle, or end of your journey. Only you will know, as you learn how you process your experiences and dreams. Because, after all, this is always and ultimately about you, your journey, your process, your speed.

Groups

Oh, the joys of a group of like-minded people! And I am not referring to 12-step or group therapy or any of that, although there are principles that transcend every program name, title, or demographic, and that apply to every endeavor. I am referring to a group of creative people sharing their ups and down, the ins and outs, the unique qualities that help or hinder someone as they go forth into the possible.

Even if you are creating your first business—traditional brick-and-mortar, Internet, service, or "at home"—the same principles come into play. You are dreaming. Your dream is to be of service. To create your restaurant, bar, invention, whatever it may be, to create gainful employment for yourself and others and to offer your product or service to the world to improve the quality of others' lives, too. Without the dream, I don't know where any of us would be.

With the innovations in technology, "group" doesn't always mean we drive to a room with a coffee machine and folding chairs. A group is now often a conference call, and whether it's traditional business or creating music, a group of like-minded people can be an excellent resource. A good moderator or leader is a gift. A godsend. But not all moderators are as good as they think they are. Or as good a fit as you hope they will be. In addition to being part of the group, you are also learning from each person there. The annoying know-it-all (who can't get going) may remind you of yourself and without realizing it, they annoy you because it is too close to your truth. The passive, scared person might bring up those fears within you. How far removed from the scared place are you or is it still in your rearview mirror? Is it close enough that you still get scared? Do you resent the over-confident, I-have-the-world-on-a-string person because that's who you hope to be and they are already there? Every stereotype and archetype is going to present itself. The reason caricatures endure is that they are true to life. We would like to think the problem in the room is this cast of characters. We don't like to think that the character with a few issues just might be us.

It very well might be us.

If you are participating and paying attention and find that at the end of the session, you are not feeling good about it or the process, then it is time to listen to your inner voice. Not every group is going to fill your needs. Sometimes the group members are at a different place than you are—ahead or behind.

Sometimes you are dealing with a leader who has unfulfilled issues. We've all been in a room where the leader has a darling or scapegoat. If it doesn't feel right, ask yourself why. If the why has to do with how the leader treats people, you have your answer, and it is a good one. If you don't feel safe, you will have a hard time trusting and growing. That is just common sense. If you are uncomfortable because you are out of your element, then there are other questions to begin your work. You selected this. Was it from aspirational thoughts? Did the description sound right, but the approach felt wrong? Is the time not convenient for you and it is too much of a push to be there?

These questions will all tell you about yourself.

Uncomfortable with the leaders? Then you are aware of your comfort zones and what you need to flourish.

Out of your element? Is it because you were hoping to rise to the occasion or you thought you were further along than you are? Is it worth staying to be sparked into greatness or are you out of your league? What did it feel like when you thought you were up there with them? And how did it feel when you realized you needed to rethink it? Do they lecture and you need an interpersonal approach? That's also good info.

Is it not convenient? This is a hard one, and only you will know the answer. None of us seems to have enough time in our day. None of us appears to get enough sleep. All of us say we want to change, but the magic fairy wand seems to be broken. Or lost. Or retired. So the hope of waking up magically in a new place needs to stay in the fairy tales of our youth.

If we aren't willing to be inconvenienced, then how badly do we really want to change? Or do we only think it's something we want?

Only you know that.

Skype

I'm a girl who loves her Skype with my friends throughout the four corners of the world. To me, it seems to offer the best of one-on-one and can be combined to do groups. Granted, you need to know your comfort level with technology. You need to be aware of your comfort level with the Internet, computer, software, and automatic updating, and how to proceed when the headset isn't working, when the other party can't hear you, when there are time zone mix-ups, and when the odd surprise happens. Because it will. And because it does.

But the advantage is we are no longer limited by time, geography, travel expense, and availability when we are part of a Skype one-on-one or group. The expert can be anywhere, and all we need is a computer and Wi-Fi or an Internet connection.

I learned of an avid bicycling enthusiast whose love for the sport led to his helping other people via a blog, which became a service, which has become an extraordinary business for this gentleman. The fact that he is in Australia is not an issue.

That is the magic.

It sounds repetitive, but you and your reactions are teaching you about yourself, and about how you are processing. Skype will, too. You will discover your inner techie. You will find out how patient you are. You will see how good you are at cleaning your office in five minutes so that when the call begins, your workspace appears professional. (No one needs to know that everything that was just lying about randomly has been stuffed into a banker box.)

And sometimes having to do the quick clean too many times can bring up other questions for you to answer, too.

Webinar

All the world loves a webinar. Easy to see why. Record it once. Offer it again. It is the modern equivalent of Spanish lessons on tape.

That sounds very cheeky and disrespectful, but it is not meant that way in the least. Good stuff is good stuff. Live or recorded, the message and wisdom contained therein, are all still relevant. And furthermore, don't we want the people, the experts, the visionaries, to be out there delving into new fields, asking new questions, thinking new thoughts, and addressing new topics? Isn't that what drew us to them initially?

Oddly enough, webinars require a fair amount of self-discipline. When you are front of someone who can see you (or most of you), we must have what I call party manners. We look at them. We listen to them. We take notes. We write things down. With a webinar, there might be slides. There might not. Or there might be a few.

It is so easy with all our technology to have the webinar on our computer, laptop, tablet, or even a phone. With these delightful toys that can multitask so well, especially in listen-only mode, it's tempting to check Facebook, clean out emails, pin some things to Pinterest, or check Amazon for those shoes, books, or another thing you forgot to order. The temptation is too often too tempting, and we don't say no.

We all firmly believe in our ability to multitask. We wear our capacity to multitask like a badge of honor. And more and more, it's becoming apparent that we humans have overestimated our ability to process information, and that perhaps our ability to multitask is greater in our minds than in reality.

I could miss the secret to the universe while I am reserving the book for my book club meeting from the library. That task certainly isn't life or death, but it is distracting. I find I end up listening a second time because I have missed some fabulous piece of information. So in "saving time," I have doubled the amount of time I planned to attend the event. The only person I have robbed is myself. I have compromised my time, my learning, my sense of self (since I've learned I can't walk and chew gum as well as I thought I could), and my peace of mind (since the question of "What else am I not doing well?" might rear its ugly head).

Know yourself. I know for me when a webinar is primarily lecture-focused, I need to sit in a still, quiet place, with no toys or gadget space, and limit what I have before me to a beverage, a pen or pencil, and a few pieces of paper.

Knowing how you can best absorb the wisdom of the webinar will be your discovery.

Teleconferences

Somehow, these feel old and new at the same time. The best feature is they are readily available if you are at home or office. Even on the road. All you need is a phone of some sort. The very freedom of the event is something to be aware of. Again, it is all about how each of us processes things. In an information setting, where technical information or technology is being discussed, and materials, PDFs, schematics, and other such items are sent before the call; teleconferences can be a tremendous help. Brilliant minds from the furthest reaches can gather to ponder the possibilities or to finesse the questions at hand.

With teleconferences, I think you need your "A game" at all times. It is also an option when used for a group setting, can be beautiful and liberating, with great camaraderie or a degree of anonymity, as desired. This is an excellent vehicle for a master-mind group, philosophy, or a support system group. To flesh out or follow up on thoughts in a safe environment. All participants at some level have been prescreened. In one group I have belonged to, each of us is in a different state. The input from those people in differing regions is both helpful and eye-opening. It provides a viewpoint that I do not have access to, and that gives it great value.

Of course, since it is without visual accountability and technology is ever-present, there are moments when it is all too easy to not be present. To weave in and out of the discussion, if you so choose.

One-Day Seminars

Don't we all love the idea that, in just a few short hours, we can have the secrets of the universe laid before us?

To me, that is the appeal of a one-day seminar. The ability to go in green and come out seasoned. Depending on the topic, that very well might happen. Depending on where you are in your growth, development, or search, anything could happen. It also can spark you to new heights or challenge your mindset.

What's wonderful is that it is fast and furious, fun and fact-filled, populated by different people and opinions, and gives you new perspectives. The pace is quick, with breaks for the necessities. My internal clock slows down at 3 p.m., so again, know yourself. And if you go fuzzy mid-morning, know that taking copious notes might help you power through. Or maybe this is a double-shot-of-espresso day.

Of course, if you are going to clear your calendar for one whole day, with all the stress, rescheduling, and other questions that come into play, you might want to consider longer options. Fully removing yourself from the day-to-day things that must be done and are just temporarily sidelined might be more appealing. Then again, the luxury of a drive to a destination allows time to dream and then time to absorb with a minimum of expense. Which brings us to the luxury model of experiences.

Retreat

I am always of two minds about retreats. One is that I go and am enthused, energized, and ready to take on the world. The other is that, by Tuesday, I'm trying to remember how I thought I could incorporate this into my life and still do everything else.

The advantage of a retreat is it allows your mind to be clear and unfettered. To dream again and think. Of course, that comes with other issues as well, but a retreat can be an excellent escape as well as a fabulous way to recharge. The longer the time, the stronger the imprint and message, the more time you have to live in your thoughts.

There are downsides, too. Depending on where you live and where the retreat is held, there may be the added expenses of transportation and the need to determine if car or air is the most practical way to get there, figuring in the factors of time and money. There is the cost of a hotel or other accommodations to consider, and you may have to pay for meals if they aren't included. And more and more important nowadays: Is coffee included or is there at least a nearby concession? For some, a new wardrobe might be needed (emotionally, if not actually). There might be business cards, computer or tablet needs, software upgrades or other technology matters to consider. If you prefer a spiral notebook, bring it, since old-school options still work.

In Summary

No matter which option you choose, know how you will work with it. Know your strengths and your weaknesses. If you get distracted, but a webinar is the only way to access those materials, have a plan to stay focused. It might mean sitting alone in a room with no distractions or going to an office lobby or outside space where you will stay on topic.

The same goes for a teleconference. If you are not required to be interactive and will have your computer on, can you resist its siren song to check emails or Facebook? Studies are out about the addictive nature of social media. We are after all, very human. Our humanity is what allows us to dream our dreams and create as we do. But sometimes it's nice to know ourselves well. This might just be one of those times.

Harvard University recently did a study to look at why social media platforms are so popular. And hand in hand is the degree of compulsiveness, even addiction, for many people. What compels people to be willing to share everything, very often with complete strangers? Each forum—Facebook, Pinterest, Instagram, or Twitter—allows strangers to validate your post, opinion, or share. As we seek to understand ourselves, are we asking for the approval of the crowd or daring to say who we are?

Whether I've attended a conference call, webinar, or retreat, I like concluding with a sense of "where to next?" Sometimes it is a problem to be puzzled. Other times, a clear direction I must pursue. You may like something along the same lines. An action plan. The intent to move forward. Something concrete to be able to put into action while you contemplate your next steps.

Here are my seven suggestions for you. They go along the lines of the seven levels mentioned earlier. Go at your speed, or more importantly, proceed at your comfort level. One a day. One a week. One a month. It is your journey. Enjoy it.

1   Know yourself. The good. The bad. The stuff you aren't so sure about.

2   Accept yourself. That might even involve forgiving yourself.

3   Honor your passions. Honor that not everything will generate money, but it might make you very happy.

4   Ask what your motivators are. Money? Power? Prestige? Fame? Happiness? A little of each?

5   Determine your fears. How do they play out and how do they keep you stuck, if not trapped by them and with them?

6   Identify your strengths. Decide if they play to your new dreams and goals.

7   Figure out how you define success.

8   The first six relate to questions being asked in different ways through this book. From friends. From people with whom you share your hopes and dreams. In other places and ways. They manifest in different ways, to different people, but they are questions you will be asked along the road, the journey, the experience. You will find everyone has an opinion on your ideas and plans, and they are happy to share them with you.

For some people, the journey is enough. I have been in seminars and conferences with someone who seemed to be the smartest person in the room, and when I see them a year later, nothing has changed, save perhaps for their wardrobe. For them, the learning they are receiving is enough. They are comfortable with that degree of success; they can live with it. It doesn't rock their boat or their world and gives them enough success to be okay with their choices. When they are ready, they will bloom, burst forth, surprise us all.

Or not.

PART III
SUCCESS

*A wise man should have money in his head,
but not in his heart.*

—JONATHAN SWIFT

Success

Success is a very loaded word.

There are so many ways to view success, and ultimately, the only view of success that means or will mean anything is your view. What is your idea of success, not your family's idea, or your friends, partner, or mates? What would make you feel that an endeavor has been worthwhile? What will make you feel at the end of the day and the end of the year that you have done something of merit?

I have always seen success in many lights, many elements in the spectrum of accomplishment and happiness. Success can be tangible or intangible. Tangible is easy. You wrote a book, painted a picture, created a new product, sold it, and people know your name. Easy. Everyone would consider that success.

Is that what you want?

There's a reason people write under nom de plumes. Anonymously. They are compelled to be storytellers. To share their emotions, their thoughts, their views of all that is about them. Think of poets; most people would agree that poetry does not hold the same place of honor and respect (or earn the financial compensation) that it did in times long gone.

Do you want fame? Fortune? Funds?

Because each one comes with expectations and surprising gifts, and some might say arrives with surprising costs. Are you writing because it makes you happy? In a perfect world, that would be enough to pursue our passions. It would not be necessary to seek fame, fortune, or funds. But in this world, it seems there are costs attached to everything. As much as a finished project comes with a sense of accomplishment and completion (and,

I would hope, satisfaction), is that intangible reason enough? If that happiness is all you need, you are fortunate indeed. Know yourself. Most artists, most people, want the feedback and praise of others. They need a little more.

I was struck when watching *Amy*, the documentary on Amy Winehouse, how well she knew herself. She just wanted to sing. And I guess she wanted to be loved too. She didn't want to be the star and go onto the star machine in which she ultimately became entangled. Her devils and demons were unleashed, and sadly, we no longer have her songwriting, singing, artistry, or humor with us. As she said many times, she just wanted to sing. I couldn't help but feel a gig at a local bar where she made enough to cover the rent and incidentals would have been sufficient until she was ready or able to see more.

Intangible success is being the singer at karaoke night everyone waits to hear. Intangible success is being the person asked to make the toast, because everyone knows you will get it right. Intangible success is being the person people come to when they have questions.

Success and disappointment, hope and fear, like the angel and devil, love and hate, live within and about us at all times. Do you have crazy dreams of success? Aspire to be the next J. K. Rowling? Wonderful! But also know that even having your book picked to be published might be enough for you, for now. Hopes and dreams change and grow. That is why I say this is a journey, an experience. The destination changes as we do.

That you are contemplating life changes and life challenges is in itself a story of success. Not everyone is brave enough to risk sailing off the edge of the map.

You are.

Success. The word has so many connotations and meanings. So much depends on perspective, so much depends on education, so much depends on background, making it difficult to define.

The next question is what type of success. Personal? Professional? About a time, cause, or project? Is it as mundane as clearing your desk or is it as impossible as collecting all the seeds of a dandelion?

It took me a long time to fully understand one of my father's remarks: We don't live to work, we work to live. Even now, I think of it as a little revolutionary. So many of us have become wrapped up in our professional identities, leaving little time to put the other equally important parts of ourselves into our equation. We seem to become people rushing to get to the next place as if that will have the answers, that time or place in life will be better, easier, richer, thinner, more something, expressing the disconnect we have now and our sense of success.

It seems to me that success is becoming a more complicated concept with each generation. My grandmother's big success was that she graduated from Los Angeles High School sometime just before the start of the First World War. Her twin sister did not, making it a point of personal pride and due to her ability to pass the arithmetic class. In her world, the rest was well ordained. She would marry, have a family, and be a loving wife and mother. Those were the expectations of her, by her, and for her.

It would be different for her daughter, different for her granddaughters, and very different for great-granddaughters. The expectations of success, the definition of success, and the elements that make people a success would all change. And in those changes are the clashes of generations, the new expectations, and the difficulty in letting go of past glories that hold little relevance now. Perhaps that's why we are all searching, searching for that sense of success, accomplishment, or fulfillment. Which is why I believe now is the time to reconsider the word success, to look at what we have loaded onto the word, and how we have let that change, limit, define, and haunt our lives.

Success: Definition

1   The favorable or prosperous termination of attempts or endeavors; the accomplishment of one's goals.
2   The attainment of wealth, position, honors, or the like.
3   A performance or achievement that is marked by success, as by the attainment of honors: "The play was an instant success."
4   A person or thing that has had success, as measured by attainment of goals, wealth, etc.: "She was a great success on the talk show."
5   Obsolete. Outcome.

Success: Word Origin and History

n. 1530s, "result, outcome," from Latin *successus*, "an advance, succession, happy outcome," from *succedere*, "come after" (see *succeed*).

Meaning "accomplishment of desired end" (good success) first recorded, 1580s.

However far away success appears to be, it is always in your hands. I would say that, for a fair number of people, the term success brings forth visions of financial windfalls, independence, and a bank account overflowing with digits before the decimal point. Success in our modern age almost exclusively refers to being financially well off, affluent. Yes, that is one of the definitions of the word. But that "success" has become synonymous with money gives a clue to the shifts in culture, and perhaps explains why success can now seem a far-flung possibility. Being comfortable is no longer sufficient. In a world where Chinese billionaires empty a plane to add a hot tub and private rooms to make travel less stressful, scoring the seat with extra legroom doesn't seem as big a deal as it once was. Or the airlines with private bedrooms to help passengers be rested upon arrival. Success is a heavily laden term. It is filled with hope and disappointment, depending on the expectations, and as a group, we tend to be unrealistic about expectations. How many of us have run to the store at the last moment because we didn't lose the weight to wear that perfect dress? How many times have we finished a task not to our satisfaction but enough to get it out the door? How often are we not quite satisfied with our lemon meringue pie that everyone else raves about? How is it we set ourselves up in ways that often don't support us? Or the reverse? We get up to give a toast at an event and believe it's what made the evening or give a presentation that we are sure knocks the socks off everyone in the room, but while wearing a yellow ensemble that would have been more appropriate for a different person?

Somewhere along the road, we received such mixed messages. We bought into or were encouraged to believe that "perfect" was the only way to be successful, but there are so many versions of perfect. Which is the right one? That question begins the real questioning. What is *your* concept of success?

I believe each of us has our own definition, which is why success can seem such a phantom to so many. It is why it can feel hollow when everyone says you have done it, yet you aren't feeling it.

That led me to start thinking about the differing levels or forms of success. There are so many, yet we focus, obsess, on only the financial component of it.

Let's start with the obvious one of financial success. But what about emotional success? Do you need concrete examples of accomplishment? Or do you appreciate tangible and intangible success? What about personal success? How does that differ from individual success? And aren't we all hoping for professional success? Have you thought about collective success, both as a group and individual?

Shall we begin the considerations?

Tangible / Intangible Success

Life takes many twists and turns. Sometimes we pay attention. Sometimes not.

The first time I started thinking about tangible and intangible success was when I was working with a nonprofit organization. We were a dedicated group of women, intent on changing the world—or like most women I know, a busy Tuesday. I had joined it perhaps a little later in age than many of my colleagues, but I was no less thrilled or dedicated than they were. One of our primary fundraising vehicles had been in place for years. We were well known for it in the community. We were well known for many of the things we had started and then either handed over to others or stopped doing them. The "handing over" part of projects and programs with community partners always made sense to me. We wanted our event or program to keep growing whether we were involved or not. Like so many things, I didn't question the value of our work on the event, our time, and our donations. After all, this had been part of the fiber of the organization for years.

Like many mainstay fundraisers, it became popular, easy, and fun to complain about the event. You could roll your eyes at anything from donations, to working it, to attending it, to who was there. The complaining and circumventing of the event started to take interesting turns, because we, as an organization, were proud to claim we thought outside of the box. We began to think outside of this box of requirements and responsibilities.

Sexy events have many protectors; practical events many fewer. In my city, where everybody is somebody, judgments about sorts of work started to invade the organization and its events.

One of the final straws came when a member had her cleaning lady serve the member's designated hours of work. That one action changed everything. Before that, we had banded together using donations from members, the community, and businesses, organizing them into a 36-hour store. With any business enterprise, there is the fun work, the tedious work, and the work no one wants to do. In one fell swoop, we had gone from sisters in arms to this sense of our work being diminished. We were no longer volunteers in a cause. We were the women who weren't smart enough to get out of it. As with any volunteer organization, we had members whose dedication exceeded their wallet, and whose wallet exceeded their dedication. However, this one event leveled everything.

We had all been required to participate. Suddenly that changed. Before this turn of events, I, too, had grumbled. I had joined the chorus of complainers. It was almost how we started our conversation, our working together. In my heart of hearts, there was something very exciting about what we did in a week: working around the clock and preparing for presentation by Friday evening, where a preview party that raised money preceded the opening of our store. It was the one event where you might meet anyone because you were no longer limited by committee, council, or cause.

Friendships started over sorting materials and developed through the years. At the end of the day, a significant amount of money had been raised. No nonprofit ever thinks it has raised enough, only because the more we have, the more we could do. We removed things that would be in-kind contributions for our community partners. When the event was over, we allowed businesses to come in and "pick the bones" of the merchandise for a fee. When the last items were sitting unloved, unwanted, and unclaimed, they were loaded up and sold in bulk to someone who would take the time to plan their next life.

Time marches on. The event continued. Limped along. Some years, we had significant numbers. Some years, we didn't— only okay numbers. But that annoying moment kept eating away at some people.

In any organization, there are training and education moments. As educated women—some in business, some removed from the business environment, some keeping their hands on the current trends for when they returned to business—it made sense that someone would bring up best practices, diminishing returns, valuation of members' time, financial impact, and more that I don't remember. After all, we were bright women searching for the best answers.

I was part of the process. Everything on paper, on spread-sheets, in columns, spoke to this being a very expensive event if you factored in volunteer time. Of course, that is the irony. Nonprofits run on volunteer time. Perhaps the greatest econ-omy in the world is the economy of donated time that is not being monetarily valued: from teachers' aides, to parents in the classroom, reading tutors, candy stripers, library aides, Meals on Wheels volunteers, and the list goes on and on. Once goodwill and compassion are assigned a price tag, no event is safe.

That's what happened. Dollars and cents and member valu-ation versus funds generated did not make our event shine. We suddenly stopped holding the event. Here one day, then taken from the next year's calendar. I'm not sure if we really processed what happened. At the time, I knew something was wrong. I didn't know what it was. Of course, that is always part of any organization, knowing but not knowing why. But that is never a convincing argument on any topic or at any level, and when offered against spreadsheets and facts, it can seem that you are against change, you're a stick in the mud, unable or unwilling to try new things. Or worse, you might be tagged as someone who actually liked the event we all grumbled about not liking.

A couple of years after we ended the event, some of my experiences came back to me as I served in a new capacity. I started to appreciate that all the work we did provided an opportunity for people not as fortunate as we were to shop for their children. It gave a mother who always said no, who always said there's no money, who asked how much it was first, the luxury of saying yes. All of the evenings being high and mighty, highfalutin' and beyond this work, had a meaning you could only see if you attended or worked the actual event when the communities we served were present.

Which very well may be why some people always staffed it. Rain or shine, they "got" why it was important to be there. They did everything with a smile and enthusiasm and graciousness that was not very apparent in all the time spent getting ready.

It was the first time I was struck by the intangible aspects of the event, which to my way of thinking made it a success beyond our wildest dreams. When we only valued it in financial terms, we lost the human element, which was more multidimensional than any of us realized. After a few more years, more changes began to show in our membership. Within the organization, there were multiple streams of connection and commitment, which allowed members to discover new worlds and vistas of opportunities. But often people found they loved where they were, and instead of trying on new hats every year, they kept the same one. While it gave stability, it didn't necessarily expand friendships and relationships. We created our neighborhoods, and often we stayed in them.

We all think of change as immediate, cataclysmic, overnight. That can happen, but anyone training for a marathon knows that changes are slow, small, and surprising. That is what we found.

In our search to be the fastest, brightest, smartest, most on top of the current trend or cutting-edge—in our search to determine productivity, performance, and profitability—we lost some things for which we didn't realize the value.

After years of being an active member, I became only a supporter of my beloved organization. Being less involved, I heard things little by little. Nothing bad, just the changes that come with growth and with time. There was talk of members not knowing as many members, just those in the areas in which they were involved. Not a bad thing, just a change from when I had started with the group twenty years before. The likely causes were technology, driving time and traffic, changes to the organizational structure, and the fact that people tended to work in clusters in their own areas rather than venturing into unfamiliar worlds. It didn't matter. Change happens. I perhaps was holding onto a fond memory of my time meeting and working with people I wouldn't have met otherwise.

As I think about our event, we had tangible successes. We raised money. We gave in-kind donations. We provided a one-on-one service to lower-income families. All three of those were pretty good reasons to continue the event.

What surprised me more were the intangible benefits that came from this one event. Even some of the things we grumbled most about not liking. To obtain donations and merchandise for our event, we went through our homes and looked at clothing—new and previously worn—household goods, children's items, furniture, china. No household item was overlooked. It helped us appreciate what we had and what we could let go. Beautiful, barely used children's clothing had a whole new life when a new mother could spoil her child. Gifts through the years that were nice but would never be used found new homes. We didn't know that before all of this talk of clutter and minimalist living and feng shui, we were simplifying. The intangible gift was reviewing the abundance in our homes and lives and sharing with others by releasing what no longer served us.

To staff the event, the entire membership needed to participate. Participate not only with donations but with time. To many members, that was what made it so special. Everyone was invested in the event. The newest members oversaw the staffing on Friday night, giving them their unique participation in the overall event. It gave all the new members a chance to work together, not by neighborhood or focus, but as the future of the organization. The more seasoned members provided the same opportunity to meet someone wonderful that you might never have otherwise met in a 400- to 500-member group. The event offered a different relationship connectedness that other large meetings or opportunities didn't quite foster. It provided new views of things you thought you knew but didn't as someone told you what they were working on within the organization.

To make sure the event was financially successful, we stacked it with many options to generate money. The members-only party offered the opportunity for many to purchase something we didn't need but had to have at twice the price. Perhaps the wine helped. We made our members happy as they walked out the door with someone else's treasures. The next day, we offered to students, to single mothers, to families on a budget, to senior citizens, to anyone who came through the door, the chance to find something wonderful at a pittance of a price. We didn't realize we were offering some people more than a shopping opportunity— a moment of dignity where instead of "no," there was a chance of "yes." Perhaps we had forgotten what it was like to be on a budget, a strict budget with no give.

To help the programs and organizations with whom we partnered, we looked at in-kind donations that could be pulled. From paper supplies to computers, from housewares to furniture, from books to music, there was always something that could help offset expenditures from the budget. The puzzles we were tired of putting together found new life at teen centers. The old printer we had replaced went to an office whose own printer was on its last legs. Orphan toner cartridges found workspaces happy to accept them. We were recycling and upcycling the best way we could.

The last two things we didn't realize we were losing were so ethereal and ephemeral it took a while to understand the fullness of their loss. Years after we stopped our event, we still received phone calls asking when it was or if we would do it again. We had not understood the event's importance to the community, in that community, and how far our event reached. We had not understood the depth of our community goodwill, the affection for the event not just as a bargain hunt but something that was within the community's psyche and memory. We did not realize how many lives we had touched. We did not realize how far the impact of that one event reached. In our intellectual endeavor, we forgot the heart and soul of why we started. Every event has a community need and financial component, and we had become focused only on the financial.

We also learned that money couldn't buy what money can't buy. Public relations and media exposure are different in every city. In Washington, DC, it's all about the politicians. In New York City, it's all about the arts. In Los Angeles, it's all about the celebrities, so even a cure for cancer or solving world peace might go on page two if there was a celebrity scandal. We had received print, radio, and television exposure on our event.

We had bus signs and street banners heralding our name and event, politely letting people know who we were, what we did, and how to find out more. In later years, when PR firms offered to donate or provide assistance, we learned how difficult and expensive it can be to obtain placement or position in the media, even with goodwill, even with a good cause. As we hungered for press and reinforcement to sing our praises and let the world know the great things we were doing, we learned in our city that doing great things might not be enough.

Change is necessary. Change is neither good nor bad. The results might not be what are wanted. We determined the success of our event on only one factor and didn't properly value the whole impact the event provided. Conversely, had we maintained an event that seemed to have so many detractors, it might equally have harmed the membership and strength of the organization.

What I do believe is we did not fully understand all the dimensions the event offered, and when we made the decision, we did not realize areas or items that would be lost for people who felt abandoned.

Amusingly, I look back on those times sorting things I'd never seen before, talking with people I didn't yet know, wandering with full access around an iconic building I would never have been let loose in alone otherwise, watching for some treasure I didn't need and had to have, and finding it an exquisite moment in time. As I said, I grumbled then. I hope I have learned to think twice before grumbling again.

Financial Success

I know for me the easiest and most obvious marker of success is the financial one. The shoes we wear, the car we drive, the job we hold, the place we live, all become statements of financial success.

The obsession with financial success permeates every aspect of our lives. One of the places it surprised me most is in the purchase of engagement rings. An act of commitment and love symbolized with precious metal and stone was no longer enough. Purchasing a ring that one could afford became passé. An advertising campaign that recommended a certain number of months' salary was the starting point. The purity and brilliance of the stone became second to the size and impact. The idea of a substitute diamond became acceptable, and a cubic zirconium that had been sneered at before became an option until you could get what you wanted. The symbolism of love, new starts, devotion, and eternity was secondary to the style, "wow factor," and bragging rights to a rock of substance.

Even the engagement and wedding rings of happily married couples were subject to review. The rings could be improved, augmented, and reset to show the current financial status of a couple. A wedding ring may have always been about proving the sincerity of the suitor to the family and an implied statement that the groom would be able to provide for their beloved daughter. Now it seems to have moved to one-upmanship and conversations with veiled hints about how successful one might actually be.

Even those loving spouses who reset or added to the original wedding bands out of love and the desire to surprise, impress, or express their love, do so from a sense that the original was no longer enough.

And so begins something I refer to as "gorillas beating their chests." When physical strength is no longer a primary determinant, when moral character is "sweet," but can be overlooked, defining success as financial wealth has become our status quo. Although it may have always been this way, it seems that now it's the *only* expression of success we recognize. We don't ask if any of the wealthy, admired individuals are happy. Are have fulfilled? Are their relationships healthy? Are they part of their children's lives? Are they healthy?

Do we realize how much our idea of success has changed in the past century? Do we care? Or are we just part of a maelstrom of acquisition? I have been fortunate to have known times of want and abundance. I have been fortunate to see familial financial success come and go and come. I've been fortunate by the sheer luck of birth to have had the parents I did; the family that surrounded me; the traditions, stories, and legacies of the generations. Like all tales handed down through families, I am sure some of ours were enhanced, augmented, or dramatized. While fortunes may have ebbed as well as flowed, I am most struck by the resiliency and resourcefulness of my people.

The definition of financial success is different for everyone. The fantasy—"If I could only win the lottery, I would be happy"— is a pipe dream. The majority of lottery winners do not have their lives improved; rather the happiness they had known is shattered as life changes, and their sense of trust and safety vanishes. It could easily be argued that few of us are prepared for surprising great wealth. The "work hard, play hard" approach to life doesn't necessarily teach you how to live when life becomes financially easy.

Even movies reinforce the theme that money isn't everything. Rodney Dangerfield's character in *Back to School* (1986) has achieved the American dream. He is a self-made man. He is financially well off. He is married to a beautiful younger woman. Yet he is not happy. The movie, made in the boom time of the 1980s, is surprisingly old-fashioned in that it vaunts family, education, friendships, love, and being true to who you are. The very next year, the film *Wall Street* was released with a completely different message, deftly delivered. Success at any price and the famous line, "Greed, for want of a better word, is good."

All of the traditional values seem to have shifted. Ever since Robin Leach and *Lifestyles of the Rich and Famous*, it seems no matter how much we have, it is never enough. Once a private yacht was enough until a private yacht with a helipad was available; that was enough until a private yacht with a helipad and disco was offered. Life wasn't about what you had or needed. It was aspirational in all aspects of life. Without realizing it, we were being told that wherever we were in life, there was something better, so no matter how far we got, it wasn't enough.

This tendency to define success in financial terms has been around, though, for a while. In 1906, William James wrote to H. G. Wells, "The moral flabbiness born of the bitch-goddess SUCCESS. That—with the squalid cash interpretation put on the word success—is our national disease."

Like many people, it has taken me time to realize my parents' wisdom, not only in those moments when they pontificated pearls of wisdom I was too smart to take in, but also in the day-to-day actions that defined who they were and what their values were. My father spoke of money as a tool, as a vehicle. It wasn't the be-all, end-all, does-all of life. He was raised during the Depression, one of eight children in a large extended family. He recalled that, in those financially challenging times, he was handed a list of groceries and a five-dollar bill and was sent to the market. At a young age, he knew the five dollars was not enough and began determining which purchases were essential and which were otherwise. For most of us, that's a life lesson we learn at last, not at first.

"Money as a vehicle" was harder to understand, until I realized how many people loved cars, and the freedom and possibilities driving down the road could offer. Then "money as a vehicle" made sense. It could take you places. It might not be able to take you in the door, but it offered you the opportunity of getting *to* the door. How you used your vehicle was in your hands. The perfect metaphor for driving one's life. You could drive with reckless abandon and be without car, gas, or money. You could proceed cautiously and never appreciate the power under the hood. Or you can take the time to learn—cautiously, thoughtfully, apprehensively—about your new toy, your new tool, and understand your vehicle.

My father had another great phrase that has held me in good stead. We all have had that moment, that dinner, that opportunity for a trip, the perfect something for our perfect someone. It is very easy to *not* do it. It is very easy to miss the trip of a lifetime for a million foolish reasons. But if we think of money as a tool, not an object that controls us, and we remember the value of money and what it can do for us, then every so often there are times when we can say yes. Money is good for buying special memories, for creating a moment in time, for every so often throwing caution to the wind with laughter and conversations. The result can be a special moment, different from other moments, not just an expense, but in location and nature. Used this way, money can create a memory that is unique from others and one that will sustain us far beyond the funds spent.

My father had ups and downs like most of us do. He finished on an up. He fully appreciated that he was fortunate to be able to host eight, ten, twelve, or twenty for dinner at a world-renowned restaurant. He fully appreciated that having the money wasn't any good unless it was enjoyed and his enjoyment was to spoil his friends and family. He was able to differentiate what was essential and still have enough for luxury. We were fortunate to benefit from his largesse, and I appreciated that even at the time. We knew how very fortunate we were. Although our parents protected us from the unpleasant moments of life as children, we were aware there had been some difficult times. It made the wonderful times all the sweeter.

My father also liked to say, "We work to live, not live to work." There were times I had all sorts of ideas of where we could go and what we could do with the business. Like my peers, I was young, hungry, and ambitious. My father weighed the pros and cons, considered the additional input, the amount of work, reports, filings, staffing, expansion, and while my plans may have brought in more money, the quality of life that we had would suffer, and to him, it did not seem worth it.

What my father had created was, for him, a perfect world. In the utopia, he created the office from home, had lunch with his wife, took an afternoon nap, worked with his children, had an afternoon swim, and by 5 p.m., he could have a martini. It does look pretty marvelous, and it was his daily reality. As fortunes improved, he added golf twice a week, had dinner out with friends, and denied his wife nothing. One of my father's proudest accomplishments was to give the wife who stood by him through thick and thin, no matter what, her own private, no-questions-asked checking account. She never had to ask what the balance was or if there was enough. Giving her anything, after she given him everything, made him so happy, so fulfilled. His vehicle, his tool, allowed him to give the world to his wife.

This is my history, my familial approach to the world of finance. The idea of money buying happiness has been bandied about forever. You can marry well and divorce better, but is it worth the cost? You can work around the clock for professional advancement only to discover that you not know your children. And they don't know you.

We live in a financially based society. We need to generate revenue. We need to be able to have sufficient money to meet our needs. Those needs change all the time. What we wanted at twenty is most assuredly different at thirty, amusing at forty, redefined at fifty, and as we live longer, each new decade brings new questions.

What is the quality of life that we want?

What is the quality of life we can sustain?

What are the things we are willing to compromise for financial success?

What are the things we cannot compromise for monetary success?

What is it you want? Not what your neighbor thinks, or your brother and sister think would be pleasant, but what financial achievements would make you feel a success?

A dear friend was concerned about her husband as he approached his fortieth birthday. He had been in low spirits. Finally, it came out that his great aspiration had been to be worth at least a million dollars cash when he turned forty. Even with all that he had accomplished—a successful business with many employees, a franchise business with partners, several residential properties, and all the toys a man of his age should have—he felt he hadn't fully achieved his goal. I mentioned it to my father. I thought it was silly because on paper he had the zeros he needed. He had done it. He had made it by himself—with his wife by his side through the years. My father's response surprised me.

"He's worth so much more than that. He has a beautiful, intelligent wife who loves him. He has three beautiful children, all accomplished in different ways. He's built a business. But more importantly, he's created a home and a family. None of that can ever be taken away from him. It's the accomplishment of a lifetime."

I'm not sure having money just to have money is what I consider success. Savings for peace of mind, yes. The ability to walk into the store and try on anything without looking at the price tag, yes. Being able to take advantage of opportunities that come along, yes. It's using the tool effectively. It is knowing what will make us happy and satisfied and comfortable, which will be different for each and every one of us. It is being willing to do work I believe in, so that I can take care myself. It is having enough to give to others or support the causes that resonate for me.

I have lots of china and wine glasses and treasures from the generations of the women in my family. They are all beautiful. Almost all have been used for luncheons, teas, and dinners. There was a time in my life when I couldn't get enough, but now I have given away six or seven sets of china. I still have that many in my cupboards. What one time was so important has now become an annoyance and distraction. For many years now, I have collected teapots, until I realized I was purchasing furniture based on the potential to display my collection. I now see that what used to be a great luxury of choice has made tending to its care and management take more time and effort than perhaps it should take. I come from a long line of women who love their china, so I don't know where my plates may go or if. What I do know is the markers of success I once desired are no longer as desirable.

Emotional Success

I would imagine there are many people who believe that emotional success is being able to control your emotions at any and every occasion. I most certainly have had many moments when my tears flowed. Some of those moments were absolutely perfect, some of them absolutely perfectly ill timed, but all of them mine.

As tempting as it would seem, it strikes me that being so emotionally shut down that you only provide the "appropriate" response would be worse than all my wrong ones.

After all these years, I know my emotions. The good, the not-so-good, the stuff I don't admit. We all want to be our best self. We all want to be noble and kind and good … until somebody cuts us off in traffic and a crazed fiend shatters our serenity. I have yet to reach the Zen place where I cannot react. I am not there yet. What I have achieved is the ability to be merely annoyed and let go. And I can let it go much quicker than I used to.

I realized it upset my sense of order and the rule of law. When everybody is the exception, there is no order, rule, or law. I felt prim and proper. But those are my ground rules, what I have lived by. It is hard for me to see them ignored. Understanding my knee-jerk response has helped me be at a more Zen place. I still get annoyed. I still wish they were more considerate. I still wish traffic was like it was when I learned to drive. Then I laugh because the only thing I can work on is my being annoyed. That is my emotional success.

So many great minds have considered the dark and light, the duality of nature, yin and yang, and how our opposites define and intrigue us. I think that emotional success is not stopping our emotions, but understanding, accepting, and working with them. The power we give them in denying them sabotages and undercuts every moment of our lives.

It is the choices not made, the hopes not expressed, the dreams not lived, and the chances not taken that haunt us. I have struggled with anger. I am not an angry person. But as a child, I would get frustrated, mad. The response from my father was huge, a greater response than the incident required. I learned it was not okay or safe to be angry in my family. That was something reserved for the adults. They could have rampages, tirades, diatribes and hold people prisoner to their anger and frustrations.

I had no idea that within my father's experience, he had seen anger and disastrous results from it. Like so many families, we avoided talking about so many things. Through the years, I have learned anger and rages had permeated some of my cousins' childhoods as well.

In my father's effort to make sure I didn't have this trait, he scared it, yelled it, "beat" it, out of me. What he didn't realize was that emotions just need to be. Like a childhood bogeyman, once they see the light of day, they no longer have the same control or ability to set us off. All the energy disappears like the air from a balloon.

When we aren't true to our emotions, they come twisting out in different forms. I think of the trees that grow in spite of strong winds—gnarled, bent, and angled. All life forces want to be.

Throughout my childhood, I was told some of my feelings were not "acceptable." I had no idea why, since it was all right for some people to have those feelings, just not me. I didn't know or understand that these emotions and feelings had led to crisis after crisis in my father's life. His attempt at stopping what he saw as a negative choice didn't have a context, so I could not understand why anger was a red flag to him.

It takes a long time to understand how this plays out in one's life. It's critical to understand the dimensions and reasons for the actions that allow me to move forward. That understanding allows me to let go of anger, hurt, and resentments, which can do me no good, but only keep me stuck. By no means do I have it all figured out. I continue to be a work in progress. But by being willing to examine myself, my life, my accomplishments, my disappointments, and my reasons for hesitation, I am more able to embrace the best and those aspects of my life that are not so good.

Emotional success isn't being a raw, vulnerable mess. It is knowing and understanding yourself, in your best and worst lights, and choosing who you wish to be and how you wish to embrace life. It might be the hardest form of success, but it very well might be the most rewarding.

Joshua Freedman, in his work, *Handle with Care: Emotional Intelligence Activity Book*, refers to the complexity of emotional intelligence and describes how it synthesizes our senses and experiences. That, in turn, influences how we act, respond, and learn. It is a pivotal aspect of development, perhaps up to 80 percent of what can be determined the "success" of our lives.

Collective Success

Ah! The creative force, wisdom, and ability of a group of people. Is there anything that can't be accomplished when we work together?

Some of the best work happens when we accept we do not have all the answers. Yes, there are times we do, but in many instances, the decision process is dramatically enhanced with views from differing perspectives.

But how do we claim success when it is a collaborative effort? How do we own what we love and is ours, along with the things we compromised on? How do we keep the bigger question as a priority when egos and the need for acclamation and acknowledgment are screaming for attention? Should we ask a politician?

I kid, but we all know it isn't funny. The art of collective success sadly appears to be a lost art. Political gridlock is the norm. Videos of politicians from all countries pop up the Internet, with shoes, papers, and fists flying. "My way or the highway" has sadly become the norm in too many places. The constituents' needs are lost in the battle for party.

That is what takes us back to the collaborative process. I say *collaborate*, not *compromise*. Language is powerful. Understanding the difference between the two words is vital.

Collaborate, when used as a verb, means to work with one another, to cooperate. In its constructive sense, it infers the creative process such as literary work or music or a project. In the less desirable form, it often refers to a negative action, such as cooperating with an enemy; for example, in the plot of so many WWII movies, someone willingly or unwillingly helps the other side, often the occupying side. I wonder if those WWII collaborators in war movies have tainted this word for many of us.

Compromise has many more interpretations. It can refer to a settling of differences through mutual agreement by redefining the terms or conceding on points. It can refer to both sides working through their conflicts or opposing positions and finding common ground or modifying the terms in a way that allows both sides to come to an acceptable answer. Compromise can refer to a settlement or an agreement being reached. It can refer to some intermediate solution between two items. For example, a condo could be considered a compromise between apartment life and purchasing a home. There are aspects of both the responsibilities and benefits of either purchase in the condo.

The darker side of the word *compromise* relates to harming something or someone, such as when you hear that someone's reputation has been compromised by rumors, lies, or scandal. Or the action of making someone or something vulnerable, such as when rushing storm water compromises a house's foundation. In military language, compromising means to place others or equipment in danger or jeopardy; for example, if a unit's position is compromised.

Legally, a compromise can be a settlement in which both sides to agree to different terms than originally discussed. When used in a more archaic way, it can refer to the binding by a bargain or agreement, or having one side accept terms that revise the original starting points. I say *archaic*, but even today the Internal Revenue Service has a program known as Offer in Compromise for those with a significant outstanding tax bill and limited ability to address the matter. Suddenly that term doesn't seem as archaic as some would have you think.

And lest we forget, there is a noble connotation to the word *compromise*. It can refer to the integrity of an individual and their inability to lower their standards or principles; for example, if a man refuses to compromise his family name, or in cases where the family honor could not be compromised.

Collaboration begins in creation. Compromise begins in letting go. Most interesting is both have significant negative connotations. Both have an interpretation of working with your enemy or someone who does not have your best interests in mind.

It is interesting that one of the definitions for compromise is referred to as obsolete. Yet any accountant, enrolled agent, or financial planner knows that an offer of compromise from the Internal Revenue Service can be a good thing should you find yourself in difficult straits. Not so obsolete after all.

We tend to think of everything in all-or-nothing terms. You win or you lose. There is victory or defeat. Perhaps this comes from years of watching television shows with the good guys and bad guys, with the police catching criminals and handing them over to the prosecuting attorneys. When we think in these terms, we limit ourselves to only that which we know.

I have found there is so much more than my limited view on so many topics. Yes, there have been times when I truly believed that my idea was the best and any additions to it might have diluted its brilliance. But more times than not, my brilliant idea was missing a few key steps and benefited significantly from others' input and suggestions. Errors and mistakes were averted because collectively using our wisdom, experience, knowledge, and contacts, our ultimate collaboration was stronger.

Sometimes we need to accept that the world we knew has changed, and our plans to continue "as is" are out of sync with others, out of sync with the times, or simply old ways of thinking. Sometimes we fail to see the obvious in our fixation on what is to be. Sometimes we don't want to accept that the particular area we are looking at, working in, or focused on has changed, and we have not realized it. Sometimes, in letting go of our ideas and being open to new ones, we find that we were the only one who liked the old way, and it was not for everyone, only ourselves. In being open to change by collaborating or compromising, there is the hope, the potential for growth. There is the potential for renewal or the opportunity to see things in a completely new light. When we cannot see that our own candle is burning down and we may need to rethink things, we ultimately end up hurting ourselves. When we are unwilling or unable to see things in a different way, when we aren't able to compromise or collaborate, how often does our rapport with others suffer?

In being comfortable with compromise and collaboration, we can see the constructive options, new worlds to which we can be open. When we stay isolated with our own thoughts, we are limited to our own knowledge and abilities. Our talents can be enhanced when someone outside our sphere asks the questions that spark us to better possibilities.

Collective success is crucial to every musical group, every movie made, every book written. Well, almost. In very few exceptions, the creative process involves many hands, each strengthening the work. Often a solo project's faint praise is that it could have benefited from other eyes, ears, or words.

Collective success is being part of something bigger than just ourselves. It is losing ourselves in the project, the creativity, the result. It is embracing others' input as well as our own. It is "being adult" when we want to call out "the purple dot is mine." It is looking at the greater good or result, and seeing our participation as an integral part of that result, important, but perhaps not the earth-shattering part we hoped for. Collective success makes me think of being adult, of letting go of the inner child screaming "look at me," of joining the team, the choir, my people and accepting praise or blame together.

Perhaps that is why we don't tend to think of collective success very often, but I say look at any Girl Scout troop and see collective success in action. How many of those leaders really wanted to go tent camping in March?

Personal, Professional, Individual Success

I have struggled with my weight most of my life. I have lived in a world where if/when I succeeded with my weight, my life would be perfect. I have taken full credit for the professional and individual success in my life. I have bought into a narrative that has cost me emotionally and experientially, and that limited the horizons of possibility, keeping me stuck. I have pursued and achieved, but there was always that thought in the back of my mind. The perceived effortlessness of the life of a "thin" person, which may or may not have any basis in reality, has always floated in the back of my mind and haunted my consciousness.

Avanti! is a humorous romp of a film, a subtle look at the changing times and social mores, a screwball comedy of the cutting-edge kind, or at least for the early 1970s. I have always enjoyed it, but it is very much about the illusion of appearances. There is a pithy remark hidden halfway through. The main female character, Miss Piggott, under strict orders from her psychiatrist, is eating only one apple a day and doing self-hypnosis. An impromptu "memorial" evening goes awry, and she veers wildly from her doctor's orders. The next morning, she says, "I thought I was unhappy because of my weight. I was overweight because I was unhappy."

Too often, we use bait-and-switch scenarios in our lives. We believe there is a prescribed order to finding success. A mathematical formula of "if this, then that." A roadmap to be followed. One day, we discover that while our plan wasn't bad, perhaps it wasn't the best plan, although we don't know what that best plan might be. Such questions often come disguised as a mid-life crisis, when "Is that all there is?" becomes an everyday mantra.

Pursuing a dream, even a good dream, if it is not ours, can leave one feeling unsatisfied, even if we are successful. I look at the number of lawyers I know—smart, intelligent, successful people—who leave law because they feel unsatisfied, unhappy. To outside appearances, they are the very definition of success. But not to the person within, who is ultimately the only person who counts when the question is asked. They have chased professional success, which has brought individual accomplishments, but the most important component was the most forgotten one. Do they feel personally successful? Are they happy?

Yet success is more than happiness. It is a sense of accomplishment, completion, achievement, of hopes realized. You can ask any person who loves their garden if it is successful. They will tell you of trials and tribulations. They will tell you of battles against bugs and the search for the perfect flower food. They will tell you of callouses and broken nails and dirt under their fingernails. After you have heard their litany of woes, what-ifs, and if-only, they will then tell you about the dahlia the size of a dinner plate, the apricots from their fruit trees, or the lush roses in bloom. They will smile beatifically, and you will know they are filled with a sense of accomplishment and success. Their personal success.

I feel we have cheapened the word success. If we get a good parking spot, we are successful. If we arrive on time, we are successful. We have taken everyday moments and attributed success to them, rendering the word "success" without real power and impact. Success is no longer a Nobel Prize, an Academy Award, or a cure for a disease. It has been reduced to a winning lottery ticket. Or finding a good, inexpensive bottle of wine no one knows about yet.

It is easy to see why we no longer understand success. We have diluted the meaning and now meaningful success is nowhere to be found. We have become confused by all our daily "successes," and we don't understand why we don't feel particularly success-ful. We also have become preoccupied with notions of success that define it in such limited terms we have set ourselves up for failure: If I don't win an Academy Award, I have not made it as an actress. Ironically, in celebrating everything as a success and only feeling successful when we obtain the brass ring, we have created a false sense of success that rings false, because it is false.

When the only success is a straight A report card, we negate the hard work of a student who may be a slow learner, may process differently, may have unseen or unknown home issues, health issues, or more. The C they receive may reflect survi-vorship in a storm we are unaware is blowing. That C becomes a starting place. The student may aspire to more. They may not. They may be all about sports, art, and music, and while math, English, and history are fun, those subjects are not their passion. If the only way to see success is in perfection—per-fect grades, perfect attendance, perfect manners—then we have failed ourselves, for we all know life is lived in the unexpected, less-than-perfect moments that define every day.

When my niece would attempt something, I would ask her if she tried her hardest. When she said yes, then we both knew she had given it her all, and it was that she could do at that point in time. That is not to say that down the road she might not master it, but at that point, she had given what she could to the task. I would then ask if she was pleased with her efforts. When she was, I was too. It didn't matter if she had recreated a Picasso or recited a poem from memory. Her efforts were the priority. The results might change in time. They might improve, or she might learn that this particular thing did not interest her. But giving it her all was the success. The outcome was defined by many things that were out of her control. What was in her ability was what counted.

For the record, I used to believe I had a degree of artistic talent until I attended a paint night with friends. The canvas and supplies were there and we received instructions to recreate the masterpiece of the evening. I discovered copying the selected work did not work for me. What did work was seeing my friends, laughing with others, and appreciating their artistic accomplishments. If the intent was to come home with a piece of art I could frame, I failed. If the intent was the social exchange with old and new friends, I was a success.

Too often, we link our successes together. Personal, professional, and individual success are all very different in nature. Mastering a language is a personal matter. Completing a project ahead of schedule for work is a professional success, along with receiving praise for a job well done. Having someone identify my contributions to a work project would be an individual success, honoring the work itself, and acknowledging that my work had its own identifiable style and is recognizable.

Perhaps this is why work burnout is so common. We do our best, receiving little acknowledgment, and often only hear what we failed to do rather than what was done well. Is it any wonder that Henry David Thoreau's words have such resonance more than a century after he wrote them? "The mass of men lead lives of quiet desperation."

If we don't know the song our being wants to sing, if we are lured by the music of others, if we are unable to identify our own unique beat, how can we march to our own drummer?

First Touches with "Success"

The praise or benefits from that blush ...

What does success mean to you? Your vision? Your sense of it? I have often wondered where we get our first sense of success. Is it from those first compliments and acknowledgments in childhood? When were we praised as babies, toddlers, young children? When we brought our artwork home from kindergarten, were our parents gushing and excited, or did we hear "That's nice"? How were we set up to receive compliments? How much does this play in each of our lives?

I cannot help but believe legitimate praise creates a healthy sense of self. I'm not talking about going overboard and celebrating every moment of every day. I don't believe that is the healthiest foundation. But if we don't learn how to accept praise and compliments at a young age, and know the praise is sincere and well meant, how do we accept it or trust it as we get older? If we don't understand our relationship to being seen, to being visible and a part of life, we will have to wonder how comfortable we will be when we are acknowledged, rewarded, or considered a success. If we are not at ease being in the spotlight, we very well could either deflect credit to others or find ways to avoid being recognized. At some point, we all want recognition, but if we have not been willing to accept it when it is offered, how will we be able to request it when it is needed or due?

In a dysfunctional home, where there's substance abuse, mental health issues, or financial fears, survival is often the name of the game. If the emotional cupboard is empty, how do you give to another? If horizons are limited at an early age and expectations are equally low, how do we understand success? I don't believe anyone intentionally harms the next generation. But as John Bradshaw eloquently pointed out that you cannot give what you do not have.

Unfortunately, so many do not have or were not given a sense of success, and so they don't have nor know how to give it to others. The spiral, the loop, isn't going the way we would hope.

Praise and acknowledgment foster that sense of self. In its best version, we see our self as part of the larger world and a valuable contributor. In our lesser version, we approach everything tentatively, fearfully, with the reality that anything can happen and it's usually not good.

From this perspective, it's easier to see why so many talented people are wanting confidence in their gifts. If our talents aren't appreciated and valued when we are little, how do we know or trust or believe we actually have talent? Without a base sense of our skills or how different or special they are than other people's, it is harder to get a sense of our own uniqueness.

Perhaps that is why it is easier to let other people define success, and in buying their definition, we go to an easy fix that people will approve of.

We like safety. We like recognition. And we like safe recognition, which is what the status quo is.

The catch with the status quo is that it is ever changing, and even your best-laid plans can place you in a catch-up position. Status quo or success by your community's standards can be just as evasive as any millionaire's effort to one-up his game. Housing is a great reflection of this. After World War II, and probably in no small result from the Great Depression, the American Dream was having a home, a safe place, a roof over your head. The shift from the city to the suburbs began and with it, barbecues, pools, and children's birthday parties. We went from purchasing what was needed to buying what was being sold, and as the *Madmen* TV series showed, it wasn't so much about the product as the results. Owning one car for the family became embarrassing. After all, shouldn't the wife have her own? In a short time, the kids grew up and were embarrassed by Mom picking them up from school in the station wagon, so getting a used car became part of the teenage years. Then the fixer-upper car was no longer enough and a teenager's car needed to be relatively new to not be embarrassing. I believe we're all very aware that transportation as we have known it is changing. In some ways, we are returning to a century-old system of buses, trolleys, streetcars, and livery services, to say nothing of home delivery of merchandise. My grandmother's reality is not that far from my own.

When a Rolls-Royce or a Bentley can be leased as easily as a Volkswagen, providing the appearance of ownership and wealth, then what does owning a car say about you? When these traditional markers of success no longer necessarily mean you are successful, only that you can successfully make a payment, what does having a high-end car really mean? How do we understand success when the external trappings of success seem to change before our eyes?

Which is how we come back to the original question. What were your first touches with success? The thrill of creating or achieving? Did you run a race and place in the top three or four, then learn that only first place deserved recognition? Did you create something and when you shared it, were you accused of cheating or stealing or plagiarizing? How easy to see the mixed message from a distance. In our desire to be our best, to get straight As, to be the best ballplayer, we lost the process and the steps to becoming those people. The more we have focused on getting the brass ring—and there are only so many brass rings—the more we believe that it's all or nothing, when life couldn't be further from that truth.

I believe that the sense of external success is best enjoyed when we know our internal needs and definition of success.

I've always remembered, but only later fully understood, a story about my mother. My parents and clan had been invited for dinner to the new home of friends. We children were dispatched to play and the adults chitchatted and imbibed and had a lovely evening. We were all collected and put in the car, sailing toward home at last. My father was having one of those moments we've all had when someone we know purchased their new toy. He was wondering if what he had provided for his wife was enough. He turned to my mother and asked, "Would you like a home like that? A larger home?" My mother turned and looked at him. "No," she said. "Who would clean all those bathrooms?"

As a child, I couldn't understand about the bathrooms. As an adult, it took a while for me to understand biting off more than you can chew, being responsible for more than you wanted, knowing what you wanted and knowing what you needed and knowing the difference. My mother loved her home, loved it in a way that I appreciate more and more. She loved that her home was open, convenient, the place where everyone stopped by. She loved the safety that home represented and the accomplishment that home realized. She understood the difference between house and home and wanted a home that she lived in and shared, not a house she maintained. It took a long time to fully understand and appreciate that.

When we don't understand our needs, don't understand what fulfills us, it is easy for other people to tell us what we need to do. As children, we walk a fine line, wanting to please, wanting to charm, wanting to delight our parents. They are our world, our sun, our moon, our stars. Their reactions and their praise cannot help but define us in ways we may not realize. I still remember at the end of one school day, running out to my parents' car, and my father asking what I had learned. I was so excited because we had learned to spell Mississippi in class that day. I recited it to him "M, I, couple S's, I, couple S's, I, couple P's, I." My father's eyes got big and his smile got wide and he asked me if I had thought that up by myself. I so want to shine. I nodded yes, and I was immediately filled with regret because I knew it wasn't mine. Thank you to the nuns for that fine sense of right and wrong. I don't remember if I told my father the truth, but I suspect I did. Oddly enough, what I remember most is the sense of feeling like a fraud because it wasn't my thought, only my recitation. That simple childhood moment haunted much of my life. Not in a bad way, but rather I try my best to make sure each person gets credit for what they've done, brought to the table, or suggested. My first touches with success had dual messages.

Family dynamics play another intriguing role. Every child shines in her or his own way, and parents often do their best to make sure one child doesn't receive a sense of being favored over the other. Of course, that's just within the family, and grandparents, aunts, and uncles are bound to break that code without meaning to.

Why bring it up? Every family has the character, the rogue, the remittance man. How do you process that the odd sheep of the family thinks you're great if no one in the family thinks the odd sheep is great? How do you understand being valued by someone others don't value?

How do you accept that feeling of specialness and love and success if it's tinged with criticism for the giver? Too often, it is easy to say you're just like your aunt, you're just like your uncle. It might only be in your hair coloring or your laugh or the way you say spaghetti, but if what you hear over and over again is "Aunt Sally is a such and such," and "Uncle George is a this and that," what is your value if those people aren't valued?

Our first touches with success stay with us for a lifetime. The spelling bee you won, the football pass you caught, the speech that got applause, the moment someone laughed at your joke, the cake that everyone wanted the recipe for, all these little moments add to our success coffers. They are the reasons we climb trees, take risks, stay safe. How we successfully navigate our early days holds surprising resonance for all our days, which is why knowing what you are good at is such a gift and perhaps why demanding perfection is flawed.

Defining Success and Being Comfortable with It

Ultimately, defining success is truly personal.

The definition of success changes. What was a success at fifteen is not at thirty. At forty-five, our idea of success is dramatically different than it is at sixty. "Success" is fluid.

Perhaps that is why we try so very hard to set a standard, an expectation, an ideal to be achieved. In many ways, I believe we do have our ideals established. Most people I know want health, happiness, love, and money. Perhaps the questions are: Which do we tackle first, and what road do we take?

Each of us is defined by our past and driven forward by our personal aspirations toward the future. For a while, the idea of being a wife and mother wasn't given the honor or accomplishment it truly deserved. Somehow, having a successful home life, a loving husband and supportive partner, and children to be proud of seemed so very antiquated, so sweet, so harkening back to another time, so limited. Working in that framework, it is no easy job, goal, or mission to create a home filled with harmony, growth, and love. If it were, divorce lawyers would be few and far between. And they are not.

For someone who has grown up in a home with upheaval, alcohol, anger, or other issues, health concerns, or lack of parental attention, creating their own utopia is both visionary and a success. They have dreamed and created what they had heard of but did not know.

The artist desires to create. The success is in the joy of creation, the sharing of the process, the joy of the performance. Too often, we see the artistic worth in dollar signs. I have a friend who took up glassblowing. By anyone's definition, that is an artistic endeavor—elaborate, elegant, and challenging, requiring patience, skill, and an ability to think many steps ahead. I've seen her pieces. I've seen photos of her works. They rival any work I have ever seen at a craft show or art fair. Yes, she could sell them. Easily. And generate money if that was her goal. Her success is in the finished piece, knowing it will be a treasured gift or a part of her home. The success is not financial. The success is the result and process.

Living in Los Angeles, everyone is something else. Your waiter is an actor. The hostess in the restaurant is an actress. The temp from the agency is a novelist. The makeup artist is a film director. The dog walker is a musician. Their profession, their moneymaking endeavor, is not who they are. They are their aspirations, their hopes and dreams. They're willing to forego sleep, the newest fashion, the fastest car, and fantasy vacations, because as nice as those things are, those are not what drives them, what makes them whole.

It's important to differentiate financial success from personal success from artistic success. Together, they create a trifecta of joy. Individually, they can bring happiness, but one is not necessarily more important than the other. We must pay our rent. We must get to work to generate the revenue for our rent.

But without our dreams and hopes, working to pay bills can be very empty. Performing every evening for love and very little money might sound delightful at first. The applause from the audience feeds the soul. However, without money to buy dinner, singing for one supper can become old, not because you don't love singing, but because everything else is wanting.

Storytellers tell stories. The oral tradition of generational tales is our birthright. Every culture, every tribe, every group has a way to pass the stories and feats and adventures of their ancestors. Stories are not told for money. Well, perhaps in the Depression era, stories were told to earn one's supper. But people who write, write from within, with joy and a desire to share the creative musings that flow through their being. They write to share the riddles in a mystery, or the longing in their hearts for romance, or to better understand a person or topic in a history, or honor someone's life in a biography. It is that universal desire to share. Poets still write poetry after being told there's no market. That has nothing to do with the poetry of their soul. Writers are acutely aware that when they send their manuscript for consideration, the odds are more in favor of a polite rejection than acceptance. Still, they write.

The success is in completing the story. For it to generate money would be icing on the cake. But almost any writer will write several things that they love, that are personal, may never see the light of day, but needed to be written all the same.

Each time we take on a new project, there are so many varying levels of success. There's the bravery in starting. There is the accomplishment in completing. There are bragging rights in saying it's done. All of those are personal and intangible successes. If what you have written or created can benefit you in your work or workplace that adds a new dimension of achievement. If what has been done can be parlayed into generating revenue, that's achieving financial success. Too often, it feels we have forgotten all the accomplishment, the victories, the successes along the way, while we raced to a result.

Goals are essential. Most artists would not want to have their home filled with hundreds of canvases that are never seen. A friend of mine began working in oil paints. Her work always looks natural and effortless, and that is the talent of the painter. After several months of serious work, she completed a painting of which she was genuinely proud. With much encouragement, she entered it into an art competition. As devoted friends, we went to the show and celebrated her work on display. I don't remember if the work placed, won, or received acknowledgment. I remember being excited for my friend.

It is my hope that we start to view success in many more variations and colors of the spectrum. I don't believe success is black or white. I don't believe success is wealth or poverty. I don't believe success is love or loneliness.

To me, success is knowing who you are, what you want, what your hopes are, what your dreams are, and how to sustain those as well as yourself.

Every aspect of our day has a million magic moments within it, things that have nothing to do with us, but their sheer existence makes us happy. I love to say that my fruit trees are as prolific in bearing fruit because I have worked with them, paid attention to the care, feeding, and nurturing of the roots. That careful pruning has kept them healthy. I'm happy to share the abundance of the trees with my friends and loved ones.

Only I know that I first planted them because I was at Costco, and the trees were dirt cheap. I thought why not take a chance. We planted them without knowing more than how deep to dig the hole. I didn't know I should fertilize them. There's a good chance they should have been pruned much earlier than I ever had them trimmed. And yet my joyful goof is a huge success. The trees provide privacy and shade. When they are in bloom, every bee in the neighborhood visits. During the drought, they received drought measurements of water yet still gave fruit. Right now with record rains, there are record flowers and the promise of a record harvest. My hope was to have some fresh fruit. I didn't realize bee infrastructure was collapsing and that I'm helping feed the bees. I didn't realize how lacey and beautiful spring and summer could be when the trees provide shade from the sun. I didn't know how much I would enjoy the starkness that winter offers when the trees drop their leaves. I had no idea how much those trees—bought on a lark—would add to my life. I don't know that I'm a successful gardener, but I believe I'm good with my plants. I take pride in that success.

When we hit the crossroads of our lives and start looking for new direction, knowing who we are and what will make us feel happy and successful will help us find our new path. The emphasis on knowing oneself is not just for your interactions with professionals as you seek. It is in more fully understanding what unique traits within you must be addressed for you to feel fulfilled and successful.

We are no longer defined by one job. Our lives are multidimensional in every aspect. We run machines. We drive cars. We operate computers. We oversee staff. We run a house. A century ago, any one of these items would have been a career unto itself. Chauffeur. Chatelaine. Office manager. Dreamer. In our day, we do not have one thing and one thing only for which we are known. Appreciating how much we have mastered, recognizing the talents we have acquired that were unknown only a few generations ago, are important so that we appreciate the level of success and accomplishment with which we start each day. From there, we go forth and dream great dreams. The success is in the dream. There are additional levels of success, but without the dream, without the hope, there's no starting place.

I come back to that phrase that my seventeen-year-old self did not understand, but my much older self sees as true wisdom. "Success is getting what you want; happiness is wanting what you get." It is my hope that we can create the linkage with success, desire, and happiness, and that our fulfillment is success, our happiness goes hand in hand rather than always being elusively out of grasp.

"To thine own self be true." And in knowing our own self, may we find our own success, desire, and happiness.

Fear of Failure or Fear of Success?

My best learning has always come when all hell broke loose. Our printing company used magnetic computer cards to typeset publications back before the personal computer was readily available. They were a true precursor to the PC. One mistake and hours of work were gone, without the possibility of redemption.

That first mistake was a doozie, but it taught me many things that later were lifesavers. I learned to never assume with a machine. I learned to save, record, file early and often. I learned the nuances of proportional spaced type. I learned what my personal typos are after seeing them repeated in saved files.

In my failing, I learned I would survive. I learned I was resourceful. I learned, if need be, I could recreate what I had lost. It was scary. But those early life lessons have helped me through the years. Granted, with computers you need always backup, but in most of life, you can fix the mistake, fix the error, or cover up the surprise.

That doesn't mean I am comfortable with failure. I've had many things brilliantly planned, perfectly executed, that were dismal failures. These endeavors failed for a lot of reasons, only one of which might have been my part in them. I've watched the same ideas flourish in other settings, giving validation to my thoughts about the event. Success has a million parents and failure none. However, I find answers in failure and life lessons that help us to grow towards our best selves and future success. When we first learned to drive a car, we knew it needed gas, but many new drivers assumed the gasoline fairy filled the tank at night. Or the car really couldn't run out of gas. Or the gauge really didn't reflect how much gas was still in the car. I know I have run out of gas on more than one occasion. When I was young and foolish, it didn't bother me. But as an older individual, I would be horrified, mortified, and appalled at and by such foolishness. It would no longer be a childish thing, but rather a statement about my inability to properly maintain this aspect of my life.

Failure surprises us in many ways. Yet often it really isn't a failure, but ironically is protection from our self. When I volunteered, there were many things I thought I would have liked to chair, to do, to oversee. I was fortunate to have been able to do almost everything I ever wanted, but of course, there were things that did not come to pass. While I was disappointed, I don't know that I ever viewed it as failure but rather not being selected.

Perhaps that is how I protected myself. But having seen what it has taken from other women, I am sometimes relieved that some things did not come to pass. I now see that my sense of requirement understood much but not all. I more fully appreciate those individuals who did take on those positions; I know what they gave up, what they compromised, and what they received. In accepting a large responsibility and position of prominence, these women chose to dedicate years of their lives to a cause and purpose we all held dear.

Conversely, I can look at many of my volunteer experiences and see multiple levels of success. I see relationships spanning days, spanning decades, and spanning generations. If volunteering and "do-gooding" is a constructive continuum, then I believe I've been successful in the relationship bridges that have been built throughout time, throughout cities, throughout states. My world is now bigger than I ever could have guessed. I have worked with organizations that have flourished. I've worked with organizations that have failed. Every vision is good. The altruistic goals we have are always noble. However, sadly it seems the interpersonal dynamics of any fairly intimate group will either help it build to greatness or implode through pettiness. A friend has a beautiful phrase, "the tyranny of graciousness." So often we are so busy being ladylike, we allow the little cuts to our beloved organizations to go unchecked, unfettered, and unaddressed. We don't like making waves. We want to believe that the troublesome person will embrace their better self. We don't want to say "you are being difficult." We don't want to say "are you aware how negative you are?" And then we find fewer and fewer people coming forward, and death by a thousand cuts begins. Are those considered successes or failures?

I've learned. That would be a success. My ultimate goal was not achieved. That would be a failure. If I have learned from the dynamics of failure, does that then make the experience a success? And when success is dependent on others as part of a larger effort, then who is to take responsibility for either success or failure?

Fear of failure individually is a private matter. Whether you make your goals or the goals set by another, if there is a clear result desired, you know if you've made it or not. Not crossing the finish line first means you didn't win, perhaps you came in only second. Not working on a project until the last moment and finding out it was done incorrectly is a professional failure. To me, the bigger question is about why we sabotage ourselves. We understand failure. We understand the implications and the ramifications. We know what it is.

Success can be more of a stranger. We are not always comfortable with it. Often we visit the idea more than the reality. When we are successful, we must be visible. We no longer have the luxury of being in the back, hiding in the dark, or being one of the gang. Success singles us out. Our comfort with standing alone is a big issue. If we're uncomfortable, we will stop ourselves intentionally or accidentally, but nonetheless consistently.

More often than not, it is not our fear of failing that holds us back, but our fear of what success would mean. Of how our lives would change. Of the people we might no longer associate with. Of the changes in our levels of responsibility. In living to the expectations others might now have for us or hold us to. Moving from private to public, no matter how small or how large the shift is, can be a very scary thing.

We're not generally taught how to be good winners, only how to be good losers. We are taught to be good sports. We are taught not to beat someone by too many points. We're taught to not be too big for our own britches. Through our childhood and young adulthood, we are repeatedly reminded to be a certain level of average, with moments of excellence, but not to be bragging or boastful. Is there any question why we are confused or have such an odd relationship with the idea of being successful? Or why financial success, which is a measurable commodity, has become the marker?

You can't argue that someone isn't affluent if they have that many digits before the decimal point. And so we have made financial wealth the marker of success when it is only one aspect of success and possibly not the most important at all. I know. Heretical thoughts indeed! Financial success—without a degree of freedom and autonomy in one's life—is only a velvet cage. If your work is your life, followed by family second, friends third, and who knows what after that, then what is your life? If you live to work and that makes you happy, then you have your success. I found most people work with varying degrees of enjoyment, but their real life is outside the office walls.

We are raised to be successes, to be successful, with all sorts of imprints of what that means. It is good to have an idea of what successful is. However, we have not tended to look at how the concepts of success and successful have changed through time.

With each generation, with each new advance, the concept of success has changed and morphed.

As I approached sixteen, learning to drive and getting my driver's license was huge. My father had his license at thirteen. Different time, different expectations. I was happy when my mother let me use her car. Thankfully, she let me use her car to the extent it was almost my car. Even though I didn't own a car, I was more successful than many of my friends who did not have access to their family's car. Life goes on. The expectation to have a car, even if it is a wreck, but it is your wreck, became a norm. Then the expectation shifted to having a new car, which was followed by the expectation to have a new "sexy" car. My idea of being successful was the car started, the radio worked, and I could use it. Yes, I was slightly mortified it was at least a decade old, but I had the use of a car.

Telling this story, I sound older than the hills. But I do so, because at any time, we may have lost the sense of what the current notion of success is. The very idea that success is fluid, to me, indicates societal-based success, because it changes without rhyme or reason, is unable to provide long-term, emotionally fulfilling success. Which very well might be the reason so many of us wonder what it means to be successful. If success is based on meeting needs, that's a very different standard than success as a lifestyle lived, a completely different standard than position in the community, which can also be far removed from financial or property success. We've all heard people say they are house rich and cash poor. We've all heard people say they'd love to go on vacation, but they're needed too much at work. We've all known someone who stayed in an arrangement, relationship, or marriage even when they knew it was no longer healthy, because the position society had conferred upon them through that relationship would be lost, and that position had become linked with their identity. All of these refer to outward-focused success rather than inward-understood fulfillment.

The markers keep getting moved, and we continue to wonder what the next one will be. Our current obsession is with education and collecting degrees, letters, titles, as if enough of these will be the answer to the universe. By elevating one form of knowledge, I believe we accidentally negate other forms of knowledge and talent.

Anyone who has ever had issues with the pipes in their home knows the value of a good plumber. Forgotten in the porcelain void is an understanding of water force, pressure, angles, slope, runoff, interconnecting pipes, linkage to city systems, lot level gradation, water flow, chemistry, toxicity levels, and fumes, along with time management, problem solving, public relations, mind-reading, budgeting, bill collecting, and goodwill. Services usually provided in under one hour.

In reducing a profession to the problem, we have forgotten the skills, knowledge, and talent brought forward to solving it.

Last Thoughts or Here's to Your Starting Place

There is no beginning to an end
But there is a beginning and an end
To beginning.

—GERTRUDE STEIN

When I started this work, it was because I had questions. In looking at my life, I had questions. In looking at how I processed, I had questions. In looking at how I approached things, I had questions. In my naiveté, I thought I had my answers. During this time, I discovered a fascination with the questions, a gift I believe is good for all. In ebullient enthusiasm, I sent forth my work for reading.

The responses I received back were overall kind and greatly encouraging. But it raised a question all my questioning had failed to raise. I was so focused on understanding the what and the how to, I forgot to ask where.

Where was my search taking me? Where did I see my life going? What was all this new knowledge going to help me with or help me become?

I had to admit it was an excellent question.

I have discussed my hopes at the very start of this book. An old phrase that has taken me a long time to understand and one that I quoted earlier—"Success is getting what you want; happiness is wanting what you get"—was one of my guiding stars.

I had unintentionally fallen so in love with my questions I forgot to ask myself where I was going and what I wanted to do.

As children, we have a few role models, so we have a few ready answers when we are asked, "What do you want to be when you grow up?" Cowboy. Doctor. Mother. Racecar Driver. They are easily understood roles for a child. We've seen them on TV and they either look fun or appeal to something in us. As we grow older, we understand that we need a job and some form of economic force to generate money and be part of society. In other words, we must grow up and leave our parents' home. Sometimes we delay it and sometimes we are ready to run out the door the first moment we can. However, I believe it would be fair to say the person who knows exactly what they want to do with their life the day they turn eighteen is a rare exception. To those who have had such clarity of thought and purpose, I salute you and appreciate the purity within your being to know who you are so young.

Ongoing education, be it college or vocational school, opens our eyes to possibilities, some practical and some not. I may have studied geology and have touched the San Andreas Fault, but the class whetted my intellectual curiosity, not a desire to go into the strata of the earth. I think of many of the classes I took and appreciate their opening my intellectual curiosity, but none called to a passion within, leaving me and every woman of a certain age, a personal dilemma. Not only women, although it often struck me you could tell when a woman graduated from college or struck out on her own by the career choice she made. The girls from the 1960s went towards education, while the women of the '70s went towards law, the ladies of the 1980s moved towards finance, banking, or brokering, and the women of the 1990s went to real estate. No surprise that turn-of-the-century opportunities in Internet companies were a draw, and the following decade, social media managers and entrepreneurs appeared to be the next direction. The reason I focused on women in this observation is that, for the most part, all avenues have been opened for the men to explore, whereas women tend to explore an area in a pack for safety, sisterhood, and impact. In fairness, the men have the same dilemmas as to where to take their lives, but again, men have traditionally appeared to have more options and flexibility than women. Although anyone who has ever watched the *Meet the Fockers* movie franchise can appreciate the running joke that Gaylord is "just" a nurse, a male nurse.

While it would seem that life should be easier given more choices, sadly it appears that more choices do not necessarily make us happier. Studies show we are wired for quick decisions. Too many options, from cereal to tea to life choices, have led us to question every choice because we realize there are so many options possible.

Even finding what we believe will make us happiest comes with one million questions, ranging from frivolous to thought provoking to scaring ourselves away from our dream. Perhaps that is why, after all my questions, I failed to ask myself the important question, the question that seems such a no-brainer, that it was hard to believe I hadn't asked it. After meditating on it all, it was evident I was dancing around the question of success. A question I believe is hard for any of us to answer honestly or fully or without inner judgment or outer expectations.

Starting with the wave of baby boomers, generations have been labeled with cute marketing names. Gen X. Gen Y. Millennial. All fine and dandy to describe a growth spurt, but what is more noteworthy are the intergenerational shifts in hopes, expectations, dreams, values, and approaches to life. We are each of us a product of our generation, of the forces and factors current during our childhood, adolescence, and young adulthood. The sense of what made one successful in the 1950s has a different resonance fifty or sixty years later.

Which is to me, why the question of success is ever more important and we need to understand it in more than an iconic or isolated context. It is my hope that each of us can understand what makes us individually happy and what gives us the individual feeling of success, in a way that cannot be limited or destroyed by the capricious whims of finance. It is my hope that each of us can know ourselves so well that we know when to stand our own ground or when to say when, and in so doing, have no regrets or hesitation. It is my hope that whether you have a chauffeured Rolls-Royce or a bus pass to go to work, you enjoy your travels to your professional location. For too long, I believe too many have looked outward for that which will help them feel secure and fulfilled. I hope that I have raised some questions to help you find not only your success, but your happiness, and in so doing, help your life be more fulfilled. I can only ask questions. The hard work is always from within, taking the time to really ask what it is we individually need and want and aspire to, at the same time looking at the dark side of our fears, needs, and wants.

If this helps you ask yourself the questions you need for your internal work, I am happy. I hope that you obtain success in getting what you want. More importantly, I hope you find the happiness in wanting what you get, and the two are linked in a constructive circle that surrounds you and allows you to live your life with fullness and purpose. Ultimately, isn't that what each of us really wants for the other?

ACKNOWLEDGMENTS

I have read many a list of acknowledgments, but until now, I hadn't fully appreciated the team of superlative souls that shepherd each work to completion. I have been blessed to encounter the people I have on my journey. A simple suggestion from Leigh Perry introduced me to Lin Schussler-Williams, author of 9 Little Words to Change Your Life, whose encouragement and support has meant the world to me. From Lin, William Arbaugh, with appreciation of his keen eye and observations. Then Cathy Fyock, Business Book Strategist and author of On Your Mark, who has mentored, shared, and provided insights I hadn't considered. I always wondered what an editor did other than find typos, and with Susan E. Lindsey, Savvy Communication LLC, I discovered the beauty of collaboration, which strengthened and improved my voice. To the few with whom I have shared this dream, I appreciate your patience on the longest rollout in history (maybe not, but it has often felt like it!). To my father, who purchased a personal computer for me way back when few people had one, I thank and honor you for your encouragement, compliments, and belief in me. (We named the computer Christine.) Lastly, to my sister Michelle Kelly Bebb, who often believed in me more than I may have believed in myself, I wish you were here for us to be "Kelly girls" and have more champagne than we should. I will do my best to keep you proud.

ABOUT THE AUTHOR

Melinda Kelly, a Los Angeles native, has been a lifelong lover of words. Introduced to leadership volunteering at age twelve, she found the interplay of hopes, personalities, and outcomes to be a kaleidoscope of possibilities. She often found the questions more interesting than the answers, leading her to a variety of thoughts. *Finding Your Coach: Diving Deep Within* is her first collection of those meditations. She is available for seminars, retreats and speaking engagements based upon her work. You can contact her at *MJK@MelindaJKelly.com* or *www.MelindaJKelly.com*

You can follow her on
Facebook at MelindaJKelly
LinkedIn at Melinda J. Kelly
Twitter at MelindaJKelly1
Youtube at MelindaJKelly

www.ingramcontent.com/pod-product-compliance
Lightning Source LLC
Chambersburg PA
CBHW061729020426
42331CB00006B/1160